TRUE STORY

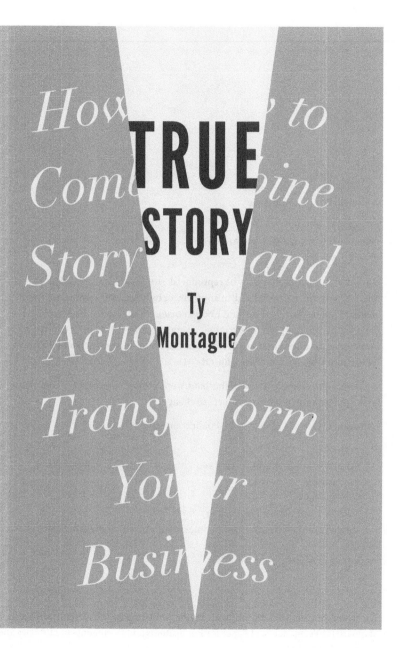

TRUE STORY

How to Combine Story and Action to Transform Your Business

Ty Montague

Harvard Business Review Press, Boston, Massachusetts

Library of Congress Cataloging-in-Publication Data

Montague, Ty.
    True story : how to combine story and action to transform your business /
Ty Montague.
        pages cm
    ISBN 978-1-4221-7068-7 (alk. paper)
    1. Branding (Marketing)   2. Customer relations.   3. Success in business.
I. Title.
    HF5415.1255.M655 2013
    658.8—dc23

                                                                    2012051719

The paper used in this publication meets the requirements of the American National Standard for Permanence of Paper for Publications and Documents in Libraries and Archives Z39.48-1992.

ISBN: 9781422170687
eISBN: 9781422187562

I'd like to dedicate this book to the most inspiring people I know—
my partner in life, Dany Lennon-Montague, and
my partners in business, Rosemarie Ryan, Neil Parker,
Richard Schatzberger, Conrad Lisco, and Tiffany Rolfe.

CONTENTS

Introduction

O ur story begins somewhat unremarkably in a European airport in 1982. Dietrich Mateschitz, a thirty-six-year-old Austrian toothpaste salesman, boards a plane for a routine business trip to Thailand. In fairness, Mateschitz was a fairly industrious and successful toothpaste salesman, having risen to the position of international marketing director for a German toothpaste manufacturer called Blendax. But there was nothing about Mateschitz at this moment that would have tipped you off to the fact that he was about to discover something that would make him one of the world's wealthiest men and that he would create a company that, if you had to pick just one, is today's best example of a company built on the concepts explored in this book. It's a new kind of company that tells its story in a new way—through actions and experiences.

The odd fact is that if Mateschitz hadn't arrived in Thailand suffering from terrible jet lag, he might still be a toothpaste salesman today. But as luck would have it, Mateschitz *did* arrive jet lagged. Some locals took pity on him and directed him to a store where he was told to ask for an exotic-sounding tonic called *Krating Daeng*. Mateschitz learned that in addition to being an excellent jet lag treatment, Krating Daeng was also prized by locals for its ability to increase physical endurance and mental concentration, making it popular with laborers and long-distance truck drivers. Now, by this time, hundreds of thousands of westerners had already passed through Thailand and presumably some of them had already discovered the restorative powers of Krating Daeng for themselves. There was really only one difference between them and Dietrich Mateschitz: where others had seen a drink for laborers and truck drivers, Mateschitz saw a gold mine. Are you still having trouble guessing the identity of this company? It might help to know that the Thai name *Krating Daeng* translates roughly in English to "red bull."

Upon making his discovery, Mateschitz sought out the manufacturer of Krating Daeng, a Thai company called TC Pharmaceuticals, and with passion and persistence convinced the owner, Chaleo Yoovidhya, that there was a vast market outside Thailand for Red Bull. The two formed a joint venture, Red Bull GmbH, and set to work on a product formulation that would please the European palate and a marketing plan to pursue a very different target: young men aged eighteen to thirty-four who, like Mateschitz, were enthusiasts of a growing movement—adventure sports. In 1987, the first can of Red Bull energy drink went on sale in Mateschitz's native Austria. The main difference in the European (and today global) formulation is that unlike its Thai forerunner, it is carbonated and contains the amino acid taurine.

This is where the story could have ended, of course. If Red Bull had been launched by a traditional packaged-goods company, it would probably have been treated like a traditional packaged good. Coca-Cola or Unilever, for example, would in all likelihood have assigned a marketing team who would have hired an ad agency, created a slogan, negotiated for some shelf space, and turned on the television advertising. But this is where the story of Red Bull actually starts to get interesting, because this is the point at which Dietrich Mateschitz reveals his one true superpower. It turns out that lurking inside the mild-mannered toothpaste salesman was an extraordinarily talented storyteller and experiential marketer. Mateschitz didn't have a massive TV budget. He had something much more important—a vision. He believed Red Bull could become something far greater than liquid in a can.

From the very beginning, Mateschitz viewed Red Bull as a lifestyle, a kind of belief system, a religion in which that can of liquid was necessary and functional. From the beginning, Red Bull, the belief system, and Red Bull, the product, were inextricably intertwined. In a rare interview with *Fast Company* magazine in 2011, Mateschitz was asked how this vision came to be. Mateschitz responded, "This is similar to the question 'What was first, the chicken or the egg?' When launching a product that stimulates body and mind, it is a short step to the roots where Red Bull came from . . . now it's called adventure sports, extreme sports, and outdoor sports. Most of the national Austrian champions in those days were personal friends of mine and we spent all our leisure time mountain biking, windsurfing, snowboarding, etc." He explained, "What Red Bull stands for is that it 'gives you wings . . .' which means that it provides skills, abilities, power, etc., to achieve whatever you want to. It is an invitation as well as a request to be active, performance-oriented, alert, and to take challenges. When you work or study, do your very best. When you do sports, go for your limits. When you have fun or just relax, be aware of it and appreciate it."[1]

Mateschitz believed from the beginning that he needed to find ways to embed Red Bull in the lives and lifestyles of his audience. Like many entrepreneurs before him, he had the vision clearly in his head, but he didn't find the right execution on day one. The breakout moment for Red Bull came in 1990, when Mateschitz, dreaming of experiences that would engage and amuse his adrenalized friends, came up with an event he called the Red Bull *Flugtag*. Flugtag translates from German to roughly "flight day" or "air show." It features homemade aircraft built by self-taught "pilots" who launch off a platform three stories above a body of water that serves as the landing surface. The main rule is that a craft must be powered by muscle, gravity, and imagination. Judging from the results, also apparently a large dose of insanity.

The first Red Bull Flugtag competition was held in 1991 in Vienna. It was an instant hit. Local newscasts picked it up, and videos of the event were passed from person to person around the world. Ripples from the first Flugtag spread globally, giving Red Bull its first taste of the power of story combined with the power of innovative action.

Flugtag was such a success that it has been held every year since in over thirty-five cities globally, from Dublin to San Francisco, attracting up to 300,000 spectators per event. The success of Flugtag was a seminal moment for the young company, and it codified a core philosophy: don't rent space at other people's events—create (and own) your own. Thirty years later, Red Bull has become a company that is hard to describe in conventional terms. Is it a packaged-goods company? Yes. Is it a media company? Yes. Is it an events company? Yes. Is it an adventure sports lifestyle company? Yes. So what exactly is the business that Red Bull is in again?

Mateschitz explained: "Since the beginning, it has been a brand philosophy and how to look upon the world, rather than pure marketing for consumer goods. In both areas we are talking about content distribution as a way to tell our consumers and friends what is new about our approximately six hundred athletes worldwide, their achievements and next projects; another band launch or song hit from Red Bull Records; what is going on regarding nightlife, people, events, culture, Formula 1, etc. So it is both ways: the brand is supporting the sports and culture community, as well as the other way round."[2]

Red Bull has become perhaps the premier global example of a business that combines story and action—something I call a *story-doing* company. Red Bull tells its story through the creation of compelling experiences, all carefully crafted to "give you wings." These events and experiences result in huge amounts of documentary content, which it distributes globally to the Red Bull faithful on platforms it owns, like *Red Bull-it* magazine and RedBull.com, and through partnerships like the new "Red Bull TV" on YouTube. In addition to the Flugtag and countless local grassroots events, Red Bull now owns a global, professional airplane-racing series that it not only conceived, but for which it also invented and manufactured much of the unique technology that makes the races possible. It owns two Formula 1 racing teams, as well as professional football/soccer teams in England, Austria, Brazil, and the United States. It owns a movie and television production company that is producing content of, by, and for the Red Bull faithful. Much of that content consists of world-record attempts or human firsts, many of them conceived of and funded by Red Bull itself. These tend to be the kind of activities that keep mothers up at night: activities like the highest BASE jump ever; the longest human flight with a detachable jet-powered wing; and Red Bull Stratos, the highest ever HALO (high altitude, low opening) jump, in a pressure suit, from a platform twenty miles above the Earth's surface—the edge of space.

Red Bull is also breaking new ground with the quality and expense of the content it is creating. Its film, *The Art of Flight*, released in late 2011 took two years and cost several million dollars to make. It takes the snowboarding movie (traditionally a pretty scruffy and handheld affair) and raises the production polish to new levels. Unlike a sponsor, Red Bull financed 100 percent of the production, and so it also received 100 percent of the benefit when *The Art of Flight* set records for downloads on iTunes at $10 each.

The Rise of Storydoing

What makes Red Bull such an interesting company today isn't that it is unique. It is that, increasingly, it isn't unique at all. Red Bull may be one of the first of its kind, but today there are numerous companies in multiple sectors that are building large businesses by pursuing the principles of storydoing—from start-ups that are beginning with a new idea and a clean slate, to large multinational corporations that are beginning to do the difficult but necessary work of restructuring themselves to behave in this new way. It's easy to see why: when it is done correctly, storydoing is simply better business. For instance, the best storydoing companies can reduce their cost of paid media dramatically—sometimes to zero.

But there are other benefits. One of the other core attributes of storydoing companies is that they have a more clearly defined purpose than other companies, something that transcends creating shareholder value or maximizing profits. This attribute often creates intense loyalty among customers and employees alike. Storydoing companies don't just practice what they preach—they actually preach *by* practicing. JetBlue, for instance, is a storydoing airline in a business sector full of long-established storytelling competitors. JetBlue's higher purpose is "to bring humanity back to air travel."[3] JetBlue tells that story by creating a better customer experience at every possible point of contact. Its story has always been spread primarily by word of mouth—the company does very little advertising and advertises only in cities it flies to or from. This has led to some unusual outcomes. Several years ago, as JetBlue contemplated expansion into new markets, it commissioned a national survey. One of the most notable findings of the survey was that it was the most beloved airline in the city of Chicago. JetBlue didn't even fly to Chicago at the time.

Fanatical loyalty and devotion like this can have obvious quantitative business benefits, like greater pricing power, lower salary requirements for staff retention, and higher employee morale. There is a qualitative difference to storydoing companies as well—harder to quantify, maybe, but just as meaningful for the customers and employees who experience it: storydoing companies have a feeling of authenticity and humanity about them that has been lost in many traditional companies today. It makes them magnetic.

There are multiple benefits available to companies that take the time to learn the principles of storydoing, and your company can be one of them. Storydoing can be learned. And once learned, it can be replicated and spread from one small division inside a company to the rest of the enterprise. That's what this book is about.

If you are a person responsible for growing a business today, whether it is a large multinational or a tiny card-table-and-folding-chair start-up, this book is meant to help you take positive action. Rather than be yet another voice cursing the darkness or making breathless predictions about what's going to happen *next*, this book was created to light a modest candle—to lay out in plain terms a rational and repeatable process to uncover and understand the authentic story of your business, and to create a series of linked actions that tell your story far more effectively than any ad campaign alone ever could. It is designed to be a practical guide for transforming a *storytelling* company into a more modern *storydoing* company.

In this book you will learn about a powerful business tool for combining story and action to create growth called your *metastory*. Your metastory, once you know it, will act as a headlamp, illuminating the growth pathway for your business. And it will function as a yardstick, allowing you to assess current and future business actions and prioritize them: what to start doing, what to stop doing, and what to do more of. In a storydoing company, your metastory and your growth strategy are actually one and the same.

Metastory: A Definition

When most people think about a story, they think about a narrative like "Jack and Jill went up the hill." Or maybe "At BP, we are moving Beyond Petroleum." These are conventional stories that are *told* or communicated through a narrative of some sort—a book or a song or an advertisement. Most of us have been taught that there are two basic kinds of story: fiction and nonfiction.

Metastory is actually a third kind of story. Metastory is a story that is *told through action*. It is not a story that you *say*, it's a story that you *do*. Every individual has one. You have one. And every company has one, too.

Your personal metastory is the story you create through every action that you take, every purchase that you make, every choice that you act on, every day, for your entire life. Your metastory is your "story of you"—the story that emerges in the minds of others as they see you and your choices. If your name is Sarah and you are unfailingly honest, pay attention to fashion trends, eat only vegetables, and tell a lot of funny jokes, your personal metastory might be "Sarah, the honest and stylish vegetarian comedian." This is the truth of you as experienced by others. Your metastory is not communication or spin. It is the observed truth of you that emerges from the sum total of all of your actions. It is the story of you that a friend would tell if a complete stranger asked about you. It is your *true story*—the story that people use to decide what they think of you, whether they want to befriend you, emulate you, ignore you, or scorn you.

Why Does Metastory Matter in Business?

All companies have a metastory, too. Your company's metastory is the story that emerges in the minds of your customers and potential customers, noncustomers, employees, shareholders, and the press as they observe and experience every action your company takes. Every interaction they have with your products or services—with your customer service, with your investor relations, with your press coverage, with your advertising—goes into the story in their minds. Understanding your metastory is the first step to becoming a storydoing company.

The reason this is so important is that ordinary people are already innate storydoers themselves. They use the story of your brand or business to tell part of their own personal metastory. Put another way, people don't buy products; they take actions that help advance their own personal metastory, and sometimes buying and using your product is one of those actions. As we grow up, all of us learn to manage our own metastory through our actions—the car we drive, the clothes we wear, the laptop we use. All of these choices are components that we know people around us will use to piece our metastory together. So as consumers we are careful to purchase products that say exactly the right thing about us. If I am thirsty, I have a vast constellation of beverages to choose from. If I pick Red Bull, it is because, in addition to quenching my thirst and waking me up (the functional baseline), I want to signal my allegiance to the Red Bull tribe. I might never BASE jump off a Himalayan peak, but by drinking Red Bull I let the world know that I might—and that I believe in and support people who definitely *would*.

And this is why for your company, a clearly defined metastory is one of the most powerful tools to get your customers to understand what your product means, and therefore why they should buy it. In that sense, your metastory defines what you wish to *become*. Once you know it, you will be able to consciously use your metastory to guide future business actions—what new products to launch, how those products should look and feel and what to call them, whom to hire, how to compensate and motivate employees, what acquisitions or divestitures to make (or not make). Your metastory is an incredibly powerful and useful business tool.

In this book, you will learn how a metastory, once discovered, can be managed, changed, and evolved to make your business and brand more meaningful and therefore more useful to the greatest number of people for advancing their own metastories. You will learn through tangible examples how businesses that understand their metastories today are telling those stories by creating products and services that market themselves with little or no paid media expenditure. And most importantly, you will learn a rational and repeatable framework and process for discovering your company's authentic metastory and how to translate that story into action.

The Story behind This Book

I am a student of story and storytelling, and I spent more than two decades in the storytelling business for companies and brands; specifically, creating narratives about brands through the mechanism of advertising.

Those years were incredibly educational and a lot of fun, but over the last several years in that business I began to feel increasingly uneasy about the growing inefficiency of advertising for brands. I saw mounting evidence that something fundamental was changing. For instance, there was a sudden and extraordinary explosion in the number of brands in the world. In 1997, based on the number of trademarks in force, there were approximately 2.5 million brands. By 2011 there were nearly 10 million.[4] That's a quadrupling in the number of brands in twelve years. Simultaneously, the average paid-media spend per brand was down nearly 25 percent from

1996.[5] So the job of standing out and standing for something distinctive as a brand or business has become much harder, and using paid media to do it has become much more expensive. More importantly, for consumers the world has become incredibly noisy, crowded, and confusing. It is much harder today for them to distinguish between products. In the past decade, all of the key traditional tracking measurements around brands have plummeted—perception of brand quality down 24 percent, brand loyalty down 31 percent, brand trust down 50 percent, differentiation down a staggering 90 percent.[6] Perhaps not surprisingly, the average CEO today is still pretending it's all business as usual—80 percent of CEOs believe that their products are clearly differentiated. But only 8 percent of their customers agree.[7]

Further evidence of change began to appear. First, a handful—and then a growing flood—of companies were building large and successful businesses using little or no paid media. Starbucks was the oft-cited example in the 1990s and 2000s. We've already learned about another, Red Bull. And today there are dozens more of these companies—Amazon, Zappos, Facebook, and Method, for example—and there are more being born every day.

At the same time, a growing chorus was proclaiming the death of advertising, and something about that proclamation struck me as wrong. After all, advertising is based on the power of story, and story is something that is innate to all human beings. How could story and storytelling for brands go away? That didn't seem plausible to me. As I turned this paradox over in my head and thought about these new companies and how they worked, it began to dawn on me that the future was still about story. But in the future, for businesses, it was less about story*telling* and more about story*doing*. Social media and the rise of the networked world were creating opportunities for companies to become much more efficient, not by communicating differently, but by actually behaving differently—taking innovative action that told a clear story and letting the network spread that story. By understanding their own metastory and then acting on that story in new and innovative ways, companies could reduce or even eliminate their expenditure on paid media. For me, this realization was like discovering the unified theory. People are not changing; story is still a fundamental part of all human beings. But telling those stories through action, not communication, was what the future was about.

This led to more questions. Could the success of these story-doing companies be learned? Could it be replicated? What was the process? What was missing in this emerging world was a playbook for unifying and harnessing the new tools of social media, software design, and technology experience and combining them with the older but still vitally important tools of product design, packaging design, and retail experience into a coherent whole. A new process was required to help any business change its behavior in multiple dimensions to create richer, more meaningful relationships with their customers. What was needed was a framework to help companies first understand their metastories, and then act on those stories in innovative ways, rather than simply telling them through the canned narrative of advertising. A framework like that would help companies embrace this exciting new future rather than fear it.

This realization caused me to leave the business of advertising and my role at J. Walter Thompson in 2010 and, with three partners, Rosemarie Ryan, Neil Parker, and Richard Schatzberger, to set up a new company, co:collective, which is focused 100 percent on helping companies grow more efficiently by understanding and managing their metastory. We set about taking everything we had learned in our previous lives and developed a rational and repeatable process—one that can be applied to a company of any size, from a global conglomerate to a tiny start-up. As we refined the process and began to apply it inside companies, it became clear to us that what we were learning could become standard practice at most, if not all, companies in the future.

This book is our view from the trenches, what we have been seeing and learning every day as we apply the metastory framework within our clients' companies and as we encounter and work with the issues that all companies face today—the need to work differently both internally and externally to become ever more efficient storydoing companies. This is meant to be a practical book full of tangible examples of how to (and in some cases, how not to) do it, built around the proposition that storydoing is something that any modern businessperson ought to be able to understand and act on in his or her own company.

Calling All Change Agents

My hope for this book is that it is a helpful guide and tool for anyone confronting the blizzard of change occurring in the world of business today. It is designed specifically for people who seek to be agents of change within their own organizations—people who want to help their company become more efficient and modern, first by understanding its own metastory and then by understanding the changes that need to be made to enable the actions to *do* that metastory. This book is also for entrepreneurs who aspire to set up a business with a clear metastory in place and therefore have a clear pathway of innovative action designed to make their story clear, different, and compelling to the maximum number of customers.

The bulk of this volume is spent exploring the framework and process. But I will begin in chapter 1 by delving a bit deeper into what makes human beings tick and how we all use products and services as a form of language to tell our own metastory. Chapter 2 explores and further defines storydoing and introduces the *four truths* you need to learn to get to a comprehensive understanding of your company's authentic and unique metastory. Chapters 3 through 6 explore these four truths in turn, each illustrated using a case history worked on by members of co:collective's founding team. Chapter 7 explores a case study illustrating the development of an *action map*—a strategic set of actions that need to be taken to make the metastory real in the world. In the conclusion, I will sum up with a few further lessons learned in the trenches.

Five Key Concepts to Take Away from This Book

1 Storydoing, not storytelling, is the most efficient way to tell your company's story today—compelling experiences are what people like to talk about to each other. A company that knows its own metastory and can translate it to action will thrive. Companies that don't will struggle.

2 Your customers are already ahead of you. They are story-doers by nature. They don't buy products; they take actions and buy products that advance their own metastories within their community. If your product or service does this, they'll buy it. If it doesn't, no matter how functionally excellent your products or services are, you are virtually useless to them.

③ To help your customers be better storydoers, to help them advance their personal metastory, you *must* understand the metastory of your own business first: what it is today and what it needs to become tomorrow.

④ There is a rational, repeatable process that will enable you to unearth and hone your metastory and help everyone in your company understand what their individual role is in *doing* that story.

⑤ Because your metastory is told by every action your company takes, ideally everyone in your company needs to understand how this works—product development, customer service, HR. This is not the sole domain of marketing, and it certainly isn't solely about marketing communications.

I hope you find the book both useful and inspiring. I can't imagine a more exciting time to be in business.

CHAPTER 1

Your True Story

Why did you buy the car you drive? If I asked you that question, you would probably have multiple answers: it gets great mileage; you love the design, the sunroof, the stereo system; you got a really good deal. These are all rational, logical reasons. The engineers who built your car would love your answers; they would point to them as proof of a long-held engineering belief that the world is a rational, logical place. The label we often use for people like this is *left-brained*. Many of these folks—engineers and others with a talent for things like math and logic, as well as many senior business executives, CFOs, and CEOs— harbor a suspicion that so-called right-brain pursuits like story and storytelling aren't really serious, businesslike activities. Some are simply uncomfortable in an area they consider to be subjective and soft, lacking in rigor. Some of them truly believe that the power of the internet will eventually make the need for story in marketing fade away. Their (quite logical) premise is that once people have perfect product knowledge at their fingertips, they will choose to make rational, logical buying decisions based purely on comparison of functional product benefits.

Let's examine that premise more deeply as we consider the original question. Why did you buy the car that you drive? The functional purpose of a car is to propel us forward at a rate not achievable by walking. A number of different configurations are certainly necessary. Family size, length of average journey, seasons of the year, and part of the world in which the car is driven all would need to be taken into consideration. Based on these needs, a few variations on the standard theme should emerge. For instance, people who need to drive on rough roads or off-road would require a vehicle that is tough, with higher ground clearance and probably with four-wheel drive. That variation would cost more to build, and the highway driving experience and fuel economy would suffer, but presumably people with these specialized needs would be willing to put up with trucklike handling and to pay significantly more for it, both at purchase and over the lifetime of the vehicle. The basic engineering problems are straightforward, and once they are solved, the standard sport-utility vehicle should result.

In the basketball-shoe business, a similar process should occur. Once height, weight, and player position are known, a standard set of engineering problems needs to be tackled. There is a natural compromise between weight and support. A perfect basketball shoe needs structure and strength to protect joint integrity and to provide cushioning and comfort, but also must be as light as possible to promote speed and jumping ability. Again, once the engineering problems have been solved, the perfect compromise should be achieved and a small number of variations on that theme made available to the buying public. These shoes are specialized, so they cost a lot more than regular sneakers, but to people who play a lot of basketball, that cost should be well worth it.

So here are a few interesting facts to consider: today there are more brands and sub-brands of basketball shoes than there are players in the NBA—over four hundred different variations, in fact. And (illogically), roughly 80 percent of all basketball shoes sold in the world never even touch a basketball court. Of the vehicles sold in the United States last year, 54 percent were either trucks or SUVs designed specifically for off-road use.[1] Yet 90 percent of those vehicles never left a paved road.[2]

What's going on here?

The only logical conclusion is that logic has little to do with why people buy things. They definitely aren't buying them exclusively for their functional benefits. So what is it about basketball shoes and SUVs that make people willing to pay much more to own them, even when they'll never use them for the activities for which they were specifically engineered?

The short answer: *metastory.*

The products we buy offer a functional benefit, but much more importantly, they are a form of personal expression. So, without my ever uttering a word, when I rock White on White Nike Air Force 1 basketball shoes, I'm telling the world something about me. When I drive a Toyota FJ down my perfectly paved suburban driveway, I am signaling something to the world about my worldview and my intentions. I am giving the world information about what community, what tribe, I belong to. This is not new behavior. We have always surrounded ourselves with a variety of adornments and talismans to signal our tribal allegiance, to bring us good fortune, to ward off rivals, and to attract mates. When we were still in caves or grass huts, we were painting and tattooing our bodies and wearing bear-claw necklaces or great headdresses made of the feathers of birds of prey. In the modern world, we go to specific schools, we join specific clubs, we drive particular cars. We wear Air Jordans, *not* Adidas shell-toes. We wear an Armani suit, or we wear a Brooks Brothers suit, or we would never own a suit.[3]

When you begin to think of the products we buy this way—not as functional items, but as a medium of expression about ourselves—suddenly things start to make a lot more sense. Of course there are fifty different types of SUV, not because of engineering requirements, but because each brand—each make and each model—"says" something slightly different about the owner. In the modern world, brands and products are language. Think of each individual brand or product as a word. We can combine these words in endless variations to produce sentences, paragraphs, and chapters. You, me, all of us use this language to tell the most important story in the world to us—our personal metastory or *true story*.

Our true story is one we each build over time. We are all born into families that already have a clear tribal allegiance, a clear narrative of their own within that tribe. Our parents' stories are usually still midstream when we are born. So our stories and theirs are necessarily commingled in our formative years. Discovering our place in our tribe and our place in the world is a big part of what childhood is all about. The clothes we wear and how we wear our hair are completely controlled by others when we're children. As we grow, we begin to guide these decisions as we come to realize that these choices are meaningful to our peer group and to our standing in that group. We learn the hard way that there are cool and uncool shoes. We learn that there are haircuts that scream *"I'm a complete dork!"* and haircuts that say *"I'm in charge."* One might say that we actually make the leap to adulthood when we finally take full control of our own life story. At that critical moment, we have to make choices.

Some of us choose this moment to reject our parents' story. If our parents are religious conservatives, we might dye our hair purple, get our eyelids pierced, set fire to our car, and join a cult to signify to the world that we are now masters of our own life story. On the other hand, if our parents are ex-hippies, we might choose to join the Republican Party, buy a handgun, and toss it in the glove box of our Hummer. Or we might choose not to rebel at all. We might choose to honor and continue their story, buy a used Volvo or a Subaru, shop at the local food co-op, and wear nothing but organic hemp. All of these actions serve functional purpose. But they also serve as powerful symbols of who we are, what we believe, who our friends are, and whom we consider to be our enemies.

The products and brands with which we surround ourselves serve as the words in the sentences we weave together to tell our story. Knowing the difference in the meaning between giving your boss a gift of Mad Dog 20/20 or of Johnny Walker Blue Label is a critical life skill. Both are alcohol. Both come in a bottle. The message conveyed by each is entirely different because the metastory of each brand is entirely different.

All of us, whether we are aware of it or not, are raised from birth to speak at least two languages: our native tongue and the language of products and brands. We have become extremely adept as a species at decoding the purchase behavior of others and using that information to categorize them as "in my tribe" or not. I can show you groupings of products and you will be able to tell me a huge amount about the people who own them with a fair degree of accuracy—gender, age, where they live, who their friends are, how much money they make, where their kids go to school. Heck, I don't even

TABLE 1-1

Two individuals: a quiz

INDIVIDUAL 1	INDIVIDUAL 2
Volvo Wagon	Cadillac Escalade
Teva sandals	Air Jordan 1, vintage
Dell laptop	Sony Vaio laptop
North Face backpack	Commes de Garçons briefcase
Above-ground pool	Apple iPod
Smirnoff Ice	Cristal champagne
Jockey tighty-whiteys	Calvin Klein boxers

have to show you pictures. I'm willing to bet that you can supply the pictures yourself. Let's try it. Each in table 1-1 is a group of products owned by an individual.

Now for your quiz. Which one is a record producer? Which one lives in the suburbs? Which one reads *Vibe* magazine? Which one is forty years old? Which one lives on the East Coast? Which one makes more money? Answers are: 2, 1, 2, 1, 2, 1. That last one was a trick question. The guy on the right is consciously telling a "money" metastory with the objects with which he surrounds himself. But my guess is you got most of these correct. And my guess is that this was an easy quiz, because you have been training since birth to decode outward symbols to interpolate information about all of the human beings you encounter in your life. You have been doing it so long now that it has become automatic. It is worth pointing out that the two individuals in question have also been training since birth to know how to tell their metastories through these symbolic objects. And so there is also a bit of a game here—a metastory can be factual, but it can also be an external construction of an idealized future state. In other words, our metastory is also our plan for what we wish to become. There is more to it than meets the eye.

Let's say the guy on the left is Bob Smith, a software engineer living in Mountain View, California. He is married to Allison, who also works, and they have two kids. Bob went to Stanford and is a software engineer working for Google. Because of his Google stock, Bob is financially set for life, but he continues to work because he loves his job. He votes Libertarian, belongs to the local Ultimate Frisbee club, and occasionally windsurfs as a hobby. He lives comfortably but doesn't surround himself with material wealth.

On the right is a guy we'll call Jarrell Vesper, a twenty-six-year-old record executive living in Brooklyn, New York. From a poor neighborhood but smart and driven, Jarrell got a scholarship to NYU and graduated with honors. He is ambitious and well regarded in his company, Def Jam, but only makes $50,000 per year at the moment. Jarrell believes (probably rightly) that projecting a story of wealth and success will help him ascend the ladder more quickly in the highly competitive and wealth-obsessed hip-hop industry. Unfortunately, because he is consciously projecting this story, he is currently deeply in debt.

Bob is just as ambitious as Jarrell. He'd love to run part of Google someday. But Bob's tribe doesn't value the externalization of wealth. In fact, Bob has come to understand that downplaying his net worth is an important aspect to career advancement in his culture. For Bob to advance his career, he has to appear to value ideas over wealth. Because of this, Bob is much more likely to spend money on exotic experiences, traveling to faraway places and engaging in activities with his family that result in interesting stories he can share with his friends at work. He keeps a low profile with the rest of his material purchases, with a strong bias toward items he can articulate functional benefits that justify the expenditure.

The metastories these two individuals are telling are conscious, but they are not strictly accurate. They are plans or blueprints for what these individuals wish to become. Each has been created to signify in a symbolic way what tribe he wants to belong to in the future. The choices are born of complex equations of background, upbringing, peer group, future goals, and current cultural backdrop. All of these factors went into the decision to purchase the items on each list, and everything else they own. If you are trying to sell Bob or Jarrell a product, you have to understand where your product fits in their metastory. What part of their metastory is it going to help them tell? This is not always a simple task, because many of these factors evolve over time. What worked yesterday may not work tomorrow, so staying alert to changes in the overall cultural landscape is important, too. (More on that later.)

For now, the fact to focus on is this: in modern business, we need to forget about labels like *right-brained* and *left-brained* and learn to appreciate that metastory, far from being "soft," is a critical business tool. To create a successful product or to grow a business today, no matter what kind of brain you have, there is nothing more serious, nothing more businesslike, than understanding how this tool works. Products that are useful for advancing the metastory of a large subset of the population will thrive. Products that stop being useful will struggle, and unless they find a way to adjust their own metastory to make them useful to us again, they will die.

The Strange Tale of Hummer

One of the best modern examples of the power of metastory on the fate of brands and businesses is Hummer, a product that went from birth to high-volume success to death in less than twenty years. During that arc, the product experience itself, from a strictly engineering standpoint, improved steadily. The fate of the Hummer brand and business had nothing to do with product functionality. Its fate was determined by its metastory.

Like Jeep before it, Hummer was born as a military vehicle, the Humvee, manufactured for the Department of Defense by the American Motors Corporation (AMC) starting in 1977. A civilian version of the vehicle, long contemplated by AMC, was finally produced, in large part due to intense personal lobbying by former world-champion bodybuilder and then Hollywood action hero Arnold Schwarzenegger. Arnold laid eyes on his first military Humvee when a column of them drove past a movie set he was on in Oregon. He decided on the spot he had to own one and personally lobbied the management of AMC for several years until the company finally capitulated and went into production with a civilian version. Schwarzenegger purchased the first civilian Hummer to roll off the assembly line in 1992 and then famously drove it everywhere, including to most of his movie premieres. Obviously, he had no practical need for a military machine or even the civilian version of it, but it filled a much more important need for him. It helped him *do* his personal metastory. Purpose-built for war, the Hummer was a big, tough, expensive vehicle for a guy who was at the time making his living playing big, tough guys in big, expensive movies. The metastory of the vehicle advanced the metastory of the action hero perfectly. And vice versa. It was a dream come true for AMC—an unpaid celebrity endorsement by one of the biggest action heroes of all time, which certainly helped to cement the metastory of Hummer in popular culture. The fact that a few environmentalists squawked about the greedy 10 mpg fuel consumption almost made it better. Who better to thumb his nose at the tree huggers than the Terminator himself?

In 1998, sensing a rising tide of popularity for the vehicles and envious of the fat margins on each unit (Hummers sold for between $50,000 and $100,000 apiece), GM purchased the brand from AMC and immediately set about improving the vehicle for civilian use. The original rough-riding and hulking civilian version was renamed the Hummer H1, and GM rapidly introduced two new models based on other smaller GM vehicle platforms, the H2 and the H3. Both the H2 and H3 were considerably tamer vehicles, with better ride and handling, much cushier interior amenities, and even slightly better gas mileage (the H3 got 13 mpg city, 18 highway).

By 2004 GM was selling thirty thousand Hummers a year. There really was only one wrinkle: Schwarzenegger was aging. And as he aged, his popularity as an action hero declined. But Schwarzenegger was a wildly driven person. He had already lived several lives, having worked his way up from total obscurity in Austria to global celebrity in the world of bodybuilding (a seven-time Mr. Olympia and onetime Mr. Universe) and then on to major mainstream movie stardom, marrying into the Kennedy family along the way. He wasn't about to take a little problem like aging lying down. In fact, he was already planning the next chapter of his life. Having watched Ronald Reagan move from actor to governor of California to president of the United States, Schwarzenegger, characteristically, was dreaming big.

In 2003 Schwarzenegger won the governorship of California, trouncing incumbent Gray Davis in a recall election that his camp dubbed "Total Recall."

Now here is where it gets really interesting from a metastory point of view. Until now, Arnold Schwarzenegger's personal metastory had been one of conquest—bodybuilding champion, action hero, cigar-chomping renegade. And while he captured the governorship by playing up his macho "I don't give a damn about politics, and by the way I can't be bought" story, that story wasn't going to help him actually govern. Californians love a renegade, but California has always been socially and environmentally progressive, with, for instance, some of the toughest emissions laws in the country. The prevailing feeling at the time among voters was that the laws needed to get even tighter. Oh, and Schwarzenegger personally owned seven Hummers.

For a while, he tried to stay on offense, using the Hummers and the cigars as symbols of his toughness (he even had a smoking tent installed in the courtyard of the capital building to get around California's tough antismoking laws). Then, sensing change was needed, he began trying to consciously alter his personal metastory—he took the action of converting one of the Hummers to hydrogen power and began using that symbolic action as a way to publicly advocate for alternative fuels for vehicles. But as time passed, there was a growing awareness that vehicle emissions contribute to global warming, and films like *An Inconvenient Truth* began to win major attention and awards.[4] Schwarzenegger realized that there was a powerful new cultural zeitgeist developing, and that even *he* was no match for it. He realized that to keep his metastory contemporary and not be seen as a political dinosaur, the Hummers would have to go. In September 2006, the man most personally responsible for the birth of the Hummer brand took dramatic action and sold off his entire Hummer fleet for a reported $950,000.

There is a saying "so goes California, so goes the nation." In the case of Hummer, this is certainly the case. Hummer sales peaked in 2006 at 54,052 units. But by 2007, the Hummer metastory was beginning to feel uncomfortably out of step to many more affluent Americans. Consequently, fewer chose the brand to help them advance their own metastories. Sales dropped to 43,431 units. In 2008, with the double whammy of gas prices at $4 per gallon and one of the worst recessions on record, the bottom really fell out of Hummer: only 20,681 units sold. In 2009, with the terrible oil spill in the Gulf of Mexico drawing attention to the ugly side of oil and bringing to the fore discussions around energy independence, Hummer sales dropped to a pathetic 5,487. People who drove gas-guzzlers like Hummer were in some quarters being openly accused of being unpatriotic. It became a very brave choice indeed to use a Hummer to advance your metastory.

With sales stalled and no end to high oil prices in sight, GM finally decided it was time to cut bait and began actively looking for a buyer for the brand. In late 2009, it swallowed hard and decided to simply shut the brand down. The last Hummer H3 rolled off line at the factory in Shreveport, Louisiana, on May 24, 2010.

You might be thinking, "Of course, it's logical for the sales of gas-guzzling vehicles to go down in times when fuel costs are high." And you would be right. There is a direct correlation between the cost of a gallon of gas and the average fuel economy of cars being bought at any particular time. However, the wholesale abandonment of a brand is extremely rare. Many vehicles with similar fuel economy to the Hummer H3 took a hit but ultimately survived the recession and the $4-a-gallon gas. Table 1-2 shows a sampling of the cars and trucks from the list of vehicles with the worst fuel economy.

With the exception of Hummer, every one of these nameplates exists today. Some of them, like the Bugatti, sell for eye-popping amounts and naturally appeal to a very rarified crowd who don't really have earthly concerns like gas money. But on this list we also see mass brands, from small pickup trucks to big people-movers to popular minivans. None of them suffered the fate of Hummer.

This does not make logical sense. But as we have established, logic has nothing to do with it—what really happened is that the Hummer metastory ceased to be useful to people who needed a vehicle to tell the world something about themselves. And so the brand died—as will any brand or business that ignores the importance of helping people do their personal metastory.

The implications of this story for today's marketers are profound, particularly in a world of wild product abundance. Today, the question you have to ask yourself is not what does your product *do*? The question that truly matters is, what does your product *mean*?

The End?

An interesting question to consider is this: could the ending of the Hummer story have been "rewritten?" Could the brand have been saved? Could it be resurrected today if a set of actions that tell a new story for the brand were developed? The answer is yes, and it involves one of the most exciting parts about managing your own metastory: *it is fluid.* It can be changed and molded. A metastory is the sum total of every action a brand, business, or person takes, so to change the story, change the actions. If GM had realized that it was the metastory of Hummer, not the product itself, that was

TABLE 1-2

Gas mileage comparison

Bugatti Veyron	9 MPG City	16 MPG Highway
Chevy Suburban 4WD	10 MPG City	15 MPG Highway
GMC Yukon 4WD	10 MPG City	15 MPG Highway
Aston Martin DB9	11 MPG City	17 MPG Highway
Cadillac CTS Wagon	12 MPG City	18 MPG Highway
HUMMER H3	**13 MPG CITY**	**18 MPG HIGHWAY**
Toyota Tacoma	14 MPG City	17 MPG Highway
Toyota Sienna 4WD	16 MPG City	22 MPG Highway
Mercedes Benz E350 Wagon	16 MPG City	23 MPG Highway

becoming dangerously out of step with the storydoing needs of its primary target (affluent suburban families), it could have architected a plan of actions to save the brand. They could still do it today. For purposes of illustration, let's build a new story for Hummer together right here.

A good place to start when thinking about changing a metastory is to identify an enemy. Put another way, if we think of our product as the protagonist in an epic story, what are we struggling against? What are we striving toward? If we can identify an emotionally positive and motivating goal for our brand, it will cause people who hear our story to become invested in our success—to root for us. So is there a problem or injustice in the world that the new Hummer would have a unique authority to address?

There are potentially many, but for purposes of our sketch, let's go with the high unemployment of military veterans. The Hummer metastory has its roots in military service, and today, as the Gulf conflict unwinds, there are over 400,000 veterans returning from the Gulf War and Afghanistan. They are returning to one of the weakest job markets in US history, so unemployment of veterans (a chronic problem in the United States since the Vietnam conflict) is particularly acute today. In fact, 41 percent of Gulf War vets are unemployed, and I'd bet underemployment is pretty high, too. These folks are war heroes. They've risked everything for their country and the American way of life. It's a tragedy that they return home to face such difficulty.

This injustice is one that GM and Hummer could act on and address in a very tangible, meaningful way—by restarting the old H3 factory in Louisiana and hiring war veterans from Iraq and Afghanistan to build a new Hummer: let's call it the "Patriot." Veterans would handle fabrication, assembly, even marketing. GM's extended supply chain would be incentivized to hire veterans wherever possible. The product itself would be a standard H3 with one key product difference: the engine. It would come in three configurations, all electric, gas/electric hybrid, and American-produced natural gas. Twenty percent of the profit on each vehicle sold would go to the Patriot Fund, a foundation that GM would set up to help veterans deal with the mental and physical health issues with which many of them struggle. The Patriot Fund would help these heroes get back on their feet and reintegrated into society.

In addition to making a positive contribution to society, these actions by GM would drive huge attention in the media. The story of the new "patriot-made, patriot-driven" vehicle from GM would become widely known very quickly. Suddenly the Hummer meta-story has changed: by buying and driving a Patriot, you are doing an entirely different story about yourself: you are someone who cares about others. You are committed to an energy-independent America. And you are the kind of person who uses the power of your wallet to make positive change in the world. When someone asks you why you bought one, you have a powerfully motivating story to tell—one you are proud to share and spread. The Hummer has a competitive reason to exist again. It is filled with new, positive meaning.

We will spend the rest of this book exploring a step-by-step process that will help you better understand what *your* product or business means to people today, what it can and should mean in the future, and how to architect a plan of storydoing actions to get you there.

CHAPTER 2

Storydoing and the
Four Truths

W e live today amidst almost overwhelming product abundance. In a world with a hundred or a thousand different versions of almost any product we could ever want, a product without a story is almost useless to us because it has no meaning. I can't advance my metastory with a product that has no discernible story itself. So today, creating products and services that have a clear and compelling story is more important than ever before. The question, with so many products and services, is how?

In the old story*telling* world, we used advertising to do it. Today, paid ads—TV spots, print ads, and digital banners—still work if you can afford them. But as audiences continue to fragment, brands continue to multiply, and the prices for production of advertising remain very high, paid advertising becomes a less and less efficient way to create meaning for people. A 2011 comScore study shows that advertising effectiveness against a young demographic is down 56 percent in ten years.[1] This phenomenon—and its partner, the vastly increased number of brands—is what accounts for the large drop in spending per brand today (down by 25 percent on average since 1996).[2] It is just too expensive to spend at those historic levels when there are so many more brands. There is also no reason to believe that these trends won't continue and indeed accelerate. You might say that paid advertising persists, but it is a relic of a previous age—the age of storytelling. This is also why we see so many new companies structured to take advantage of metastory in a new way: *storydoing*.

There has already been a massive amount written about the death of the thirty-second spot, so we won't dwell here for long. But there are a few key characteristics of companies structured for storytelling that are different from those structured for storydoing. In the storytelling age, communication channels were tightly controlled, which created scarcity and allowed gatekeepers to keep prices quite high for access to the massive audiences they attracted. In the storytelling age, communication between advertiser and consumer was largely unidirectional (the advertisers talked, and consumers listened). This gave rise to a well-worn, baton-pass process for bringing new products and services to market that looked roughly like the one shown in figure 2-1.

In this process, story got added right near the end, and the storytelling was typically outsourced to an advertising agency. In a world where relatively few people were connected to each other but everybody was connected to a TV, this was an extremely efficient model for creating meaning for products and brands. Businesses that became successful during this age optimized around

FIGURE 2-1

Product creation in the age of storytelling

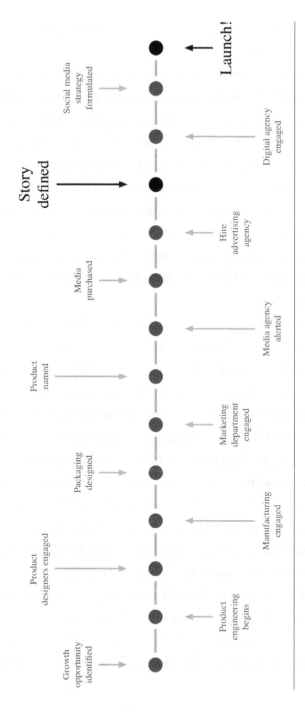

this process. They developed robust internal structures and cultures around it.

Many of these structures persist. But today, of course, the world is totally different. Communications channels are wildly abundant, and communication through them is multidirectional—everybody is connected to everybody else in real time. Companies that want to participate meaningfully in storydoing need to think differently not only about story but about their internal processes and team structures. A pressing question for any agent of change—anyone trying to start a new company today or reinvent an existing company *for* today should be: what does a company organized around storydoing actually look like? It is a question we will explore in some detail.

In their modest but, I believe, groundbreaking book, *Baked In*, authors John Winsor and Alex Bogusky argue that in a networked world, a more efficient way to market is to bake the story right into the product itself.[3] It is full of sound advice and simple but profound questions about how to think about this new landscape, such as: What if the people inside a company who were charged with creating products actually talked to the people who were charged with creating the story? What if they were all incentivized to work together? These seem like obvious and simple things. And yet, in many companies that grew up in the storytelling age, the people responsible for creating the products and the people responsible for creating the story of the products never even meet each other. In some cases, particularly in technology companies, the two groups often actively avoid each other. Engineering (or R&D) sits at the strategic table way up at the beginning of the baton-pass process, developing products and services based on a road map created with the CEO, who is most often someone with a financial or technical, rather than story, background. Marketing sits way down toward the end of the process and is thought of as an expense. Back when this system was designed, R&D and marketing didn't talk to each other because they didn't have to. TV solved that problem—TV and a $100 million advertising budget.

The questions Bogusky and Winsor ask are tantalizing and lead to others: If these two groups did start to work together, if a deeper understanding of the story that needed to be told was moved right up to the front of the innovation process, how would that actually work? Instead of designing a process that resulted in storytelling through the medium of television, what if you built a process around first understanding the story that needed to be told, and then used that story to inform every aspect of the company?

Well, first of all, to be precise, that wouldn't be a story you *told*, it would be the kind of story that you *did*—a metastory. In this alternative way of thinking about the world, a company's metastory defines and drives its growth strategy. Imagine a company in which all the departments and functions are organized around its metastory. That would be a company designed so that every action in every department helped to advance the story, every product had that story baked into it, and every customer interaction would be designed to create the maximum amount of meaning in the minds and hearts of customers (see figure 2-2). A company like that would be extremely efficient. And it would be very hard to beat by competitors who were still structured for the previous age.

In storydoing, you work out the metastory of a brand or business first. Then you design the innovative actions necessary for that story to become real and compelling for people. This is called

FIGURE 2-2

In storydoing, the metastory defines and drives all the actions a company takes

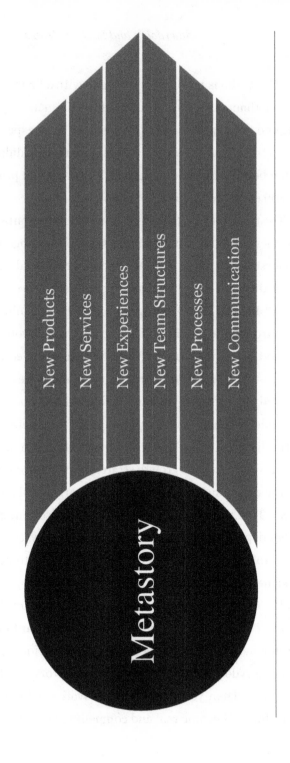

creating your action map (chapter 7 is devoted to a detailed case on this).

Do all of this well, and all of the actions your company takes become a clear and compelling story for your customers to assemble in their own heads and then transmit to their tribes. If your metastory is compelling and the actions you take to do your story are innovative, your customers will be more than happy to use all of the modern social media tools at their disposal to make sure that your story is widely known. In some cases, you may still need to use some paid media to tell a traditional narrative about some of the innovative actions you are taking. But one of the goals of storydoing is to keep that expenditure to an absolute minimum.

If your actions as a brand are innovative, if they are new, if they contain information that an individual's tribe needs to know, that individual will talk about you—will do the communicating *for* you, telling *your* story. If your actions are not innovative, if they are not new, if they are actions that have been seen before, or if they contain no new information, there will be much less inclination to talk about you. That would be considered a waste of a tribe's time and bad for the standing of the person telling your story. Worse, if your actions and your story are misaligned, if you are telling one story and doing another, your consumers will immediately know it and reject you. We see the outcry against such companies in things like the aftermath of the *Deepwater Horizon* oil spill. BP was telling the story that it was moving "Beyond Petroleum." Its actions proved otherwise. Most importantly, if your story helps to advance the personal metastory of a group, they will adopt you into their curated set of brands and businesses. They will become your loyal customers.

Act Now

Any company can begin to adopt these principals as long as it is up for embracing some real change. But if your company was formed before the world became truly interconnected, before the internet was widely adopted, before social media got real traction—you probably have some catching up to do, because there is a new generation of companies being created today that have a real competitive advantage, and they want your customers. You've heard the term *digital natives* used to describe young people who have grown up using the internet and digital media? These companies are *storydoing natives*. They are companies created from the beginning to be storydoers. These companies rarely advertise. They aren't organized or processed around the medium of television; they are built to use people as a medium. We have already met one of these companies, Red Bull. Another is, of course, Facebook, which holds the enviable position of not only being a storydoer but also enabling an ecosystem for other companies that are built to operate this way. People at Facebook use the term *social by design* to describe the characteristics of a storydoing company. Carolyn Everson, Facebook's VP, global marketing solutions, defines the term this way:

> We mean thinking about your business as putting people at the center, as opposed to the model where you used to publish messages to your consumers. This is hard to get your arms around, because so many times your business has been built around your product or your message; now you have to think about building your business around people— what people are interested in and what they want to share with their friends. This is a fundamental shift. It's not about

display ads, it's not about video ads, it's not about traditional advertising at all. When I meet with clients and talk to partners, the question is, how do we fundamentally shift the way business is being done in a social environment?[4]

This approach describes some of the key characteristics of a storydoing company. The common trait of any business that is social by design is that it has a compelling story at the center of its offering because fundamentally, that's what people are interested in sharing.

To the traditionally organized companies of the world, these companies should be pretty scary because they are more efficient. They run leaner and faster than companies that were built to employ TV as the meaning-creation medium of choice. They are more responsive to their customers because their customers are part of the conversation from the very beginning. Let's dive a little deeper into the story of how another one of these companies came to be.

The Story of TOMS Shoes

In 2002, Blake Mycoskie was a mildly successful serial entrepreneur, having started and sold a small college-campus-based laundry company and a small outdoor advertising business. He was looking around for his next venture when, by a fluke, he and his sister were chosen as contestants on the second season of the reality TV show *The Amazing Race*. Mycoskie suddenly found himself filming the show in exotic parts of South America. He fell in love with Argentina. He loved it so much that he decided to go back several years later on an extended vacation to spend more time really exploring the country. It was on this vacation that he discovered his true calling. Getting outside of the major cities like Buenos Aires, he was quite moved and deeply disturbed by the abject poverty he found in the small towns and villages in the Argentine countryside. He was particularly affected by the number of children who were so poor they could not even afford shoes. He learned that shoelessness led to a number of disfiguring diseases. Almost worse, children without shoes were often not allowed to attend school, which meant that their ability to improve their circumstances was literally over before their lives had really even begun. Between the time he had finished *The Amazing Race* and the time he went back to Argentina, Mycoskie had gotten involved in an online driver-education business. But upon returning to Argentina for the second time, he decided that he was going to sell his share of that business and devote the next part of his life to doing something about the problem of shoelessness in the world.

After thinking about it for a short time, he had an innovative idea: he would start a shoe company. But it was a shoe company with a special difference. For every pair of shoes that he sold, he would give a second pair of shoes to a child who had no shoes. He also made a conscious decision to make it a for-profit business. His belief was that charities, as important as they are, were not helping to create sustainable change. What was needed were companies that were self-sustaining *and* doing the right thing. From his perspective, that's how the really big dream—a truly sustainable global economy—could happen. And so TOMS Shoes, and the idea of *One for One*, was born.

Note that the story I just told you is the key driver of the business model, and it was baked into the company from the very beginning. TOMS rarely advertises. When you buy a pair of TOMS shoes, you get a pair of shoes, but you also get a story. It is a story about children, poverty, hope, and giving back. It is a story that, Mycoskie rapidly discovered, people *wanted* to tell each other. It was a story that people wanted to participate in and spread. And since the number of shoes delivered to children in need is a direct proxy for sales, I'll tell the sales story that way.

In its first year, 2006, TOMS delivered 10,000 pairs of shoes to children in Argentina. In the second year, the company expanded the shoe-gifting footprint, and 50,000 pairs of shoes were delivered to South Africa. As of April 2009, TOMS had distributed 140,000 pairs of shoes to children in Argentina, Ethiopia, and South Africa, as well as children in the United States. In April 2010, the company announced that it had given 600,000 pairs of new shoes to children in need around the world. In September 2010, TOMS gave away the millionth pair of shoes. By 2011, shoes had been given to children in more than twenty countries worldwide, including the United States (Louisiana, Kentucky, Mississippi, and Florida), Argentina, Ethiopia, Rwanda, Guatemala, Haiti, and South Africa. TOMS are sold at more than five hundred stores nationwide and internationally, including Nordstrom, Neiman Marcus, and Whole Foods, which feature styles made from recycled materials.

TOMS advertises very little—a few small-space print ads here and there. But the company hasn't lacked for attention from the mainstream media. TOMS has received numerous awards and honors, twice featured as one of *Fast Company's* most innovative companies, for instance. Mycoskie has spoken along with former president Bill Clinton at a global conference on poverty and the global economy. He has participated in a summit at the White House. He has keynoted at SXSW and spoken at TED. The company has been featured on shows like *The Big Idea*. And he and the company were featured in an AT&T commercial that aired nationwide.

In an interview for *CNN Money*, Mycoskie was asked about the secret to his success. His answer? "Storytelling is the new marketing. I think that's why AT&T called me to appear in its commercial, because stories get shared and spread much more than a message."[5] But the real medium for the transmission of the TOMS story is TOMS's participants. As they wear their TOMS shoes in the world, every time they get asked, "Where did you get those shoes?" they have a story to tell. It's a story they are proud to share because the story of TOMS shoes adds something special to the metastory of every individual who wears them.

When you begin to consider where that story might take TOMS, it gets pretty exciting. In June 2011 TOMS announced its next innovative action: the launch of TOMS eyewear. It is another one-for-one program designed to save and restore sight in poor countries. This marks a very important point in the story of TOMS, the point at which it stops being a shoe company and becomes a one-for-one storydoing company. Once the story moves beyond shoes, there really is no limit to how far it can go.

"Terrific. But what good does that do me?" you might ask. "I'm not an entrepreneur. I don't have an idea for a whole new business model. I'm not starting a company from scratch. I sell fast food (or I sell jewelry or I sell cars)."

How does storydoing happen inside an organization that was built for the story*telling* era? The fact is, storydoing can be applied anywhere. You don't have to start a new company. You just have to begin to think about your business in a new way. Let's examine two examples of this, one from the fast food industry and one from the jewelry business.

The Story of Subway

The first Subway sandwich shop launched in New York City in 1965—way back in the middle of the storytelling age. Today Subway is one of the largest and fastest-growing franchises in fast food, with over thirty thousand locations globally. This stunning success is due to a simple, clear, and compelling metastory: fresher food fast.

The Subway tagline is "Eat Fresh." But remember, a company's metastory is revealed through action, not words. If Subway had launched as a conventional fast-food experience and just slapped on a tagline claiming freshness, it is doubtful it would have survived, much less become one of the most successful companies in the world. Freshness at Subway is much more than a set of words. Subway started telling the freshness metastory with its very first action: it was decided that rather than buying premade bread, its shops would bake bread for the sandwiches right in the store. Even today, when customers walk into a Subway anywhere in the world, the first thing they smell is freshly baked bread. They order a sandwich. Then they get to watch that sandwich being made with other fresh ingredients at lightning speed right in front of them. They walk out with a better sandwich, and back in 1965, they also had a story to tell, because in 1965, this was something new—fresher ingredients, assembled before your eyes by a "Subway sandwich artist." Overall, a better experience, and better for you. That metastory has led to growth and created prosperity for its founders and franchisees.

Now the question is, how does a company like Subway continue to innovate around that story today? For years, like most storytelling companies, it has told its story using massive amounts of television. But lately, it has been experimenting with storydoing, particularly in its fastest-growth region: Japan. In a handful of its Tokyo stores, Subway has designed and installed special equipment for growing hydroponic lettuce right in the store.

Today when you walk in and order a sandwich in Tokyo, not only do you smell freshly baked bread, you actually watch the lettuce get picked right in front of you. The story you tell about the lettuce perfectly advances and supports Subway's metastory of freshness. And if you are an aficionado of the brand, it advances your own metastory by positioning you as a source of new and interesting information for your tribe.

Another important point about this example is that it took a team of people from across the company to execute it. To conceive, create, and install hydroponic lettuce–growing equipment requires people from finance, procurement, franchisee relations, and employee training as well as marketing. Unlike storytelling, which tends to be the exclusive domain of the marketing department, storydoing is a team sport involving people from many disciplines across a company.

The Story of De Beers and the Right-Hand Ring

A second example of a storytelling company that has begun to explore storydoing comes from a very different business. For many years, women in Western cultures have worn a diamond ring on their left hand to tell a story with which all of us are extremely familiar. It goes something like this: "Hello. I am in a committed relationship. And, by the way, it is with a mate who had the smarts and the skills to provide this expensive symbol of our bond. So don't even think about asking me to dance. I'm taken." That story is so widely known that you probably have never even thought very much about it. But if you're a man, when you think about asking a woman to commit to you, you also know there is going to be a diamond involved. No diamond, and you're going to have some 'splainin' to do.

About ten years ago, De Beers saw an opportunity to create a new cultural story and to create a new symbol to convey that story. The company realized that women's role in society had changed quite a bit since the creation of the original engagement ring. Many women were no longer financially dependent on men. They were pursuing their own career paths, their own dreams. They often supported themselves. They were marrying later, or sometimes not at all. They were more self-directed than ever before. Women had a new personal metastory. Yet they didn't have a symbol to convey this story to the world—there was no talisman to convey a belief in self, a reliance on self, and a connection to the millions of other women who were living this powerful new female story.

As De Beers was contemplating this opportunity, it also noticed something else. It turns out, women have *two* hands. With that insight, it created one of the finest modern examples of storydoing: it identified an entirely new story that women wanted to convey about themselves and then created a new product specifically designed to convey it. Almost overnight, the *right-hand ring* became a billion-dollar business for De Beers.

The key to the success of the right-hand ring was not only the insight about the need for a new story, it was also the sequence De Beers then pursued for the launch. The first step was to use the metastory to actually guide the creation of the product itself. De Beers knew that to succeed, the ring couldn't be priced like an engagement ring because for the first time women would be purchasing diamonds in large numbers for themselves and wouldn't spend that amount of money for them. De Beers had to find a design that was distinctive and proprietary, but that allowed the rings to be priced at $500 and below. The final design avoided large stones completely in favor of constellations of very small diamonds in a variety of configurations. This design allowed De Beers not only to use its more plentiful stocks of very small stones but also to make the right-hand rings stand out in retailers' display cases.

The second step was introducing this new story to the world through action, rather than advertising. A launch plan was conceived that started with product placement on red carpets and runways. Actresses who portrayed independent women in hit TV shows and movies—Sarah Jessica Parker of *Sex in the City*, Halle Berry, and others—were educated about the story of the product and given free rings. When these women were interviewed at awards shows and on talk shows, they often would tell the story of their ring. This led to an estimated $6 million in free media coverage of the story. And it guaranteed that the story entered culture well before it appeared to have been pushed by De Beers through the less intimate medium of advertising. Eventually, a traditional print advertising campaign was launched. It very clearly told the story of the right-hand ring. But advertising was really the least important part of the program.

A right-hand ring became a symbol of a modern woman who had made it on her own terms—not in an "I am woman, hear me roar" kind of way, but more of a "I'm confident, independent, successful, and sexy" kind of way. She might love men and be loved by them, but she didn't need a man or a diamond engagement ring to mark her worth. It wasn't a rejection of other roles she played and loved (mother, wife, girlfriend). Those things were part of her, but didn't define her. She was able to show off and embrace all the things that made her great. A line from the advertising campaign that was eventually developed summed it up well: "The left hand rocks the cradle, the right hand rocks the world." Wearing a right-hand ring was a conversation starter, and it enabled women to tell the new story of the businesswoman, the fashion designer, the architect.

It was interesting (perhaps ironic) that over time, almost 40 percent of right-hand rings were bought by men as a gift to the women in their lives as their way of acknowledging that they weren't just great moms and wives but awesome women in their own right. It gave men another (less traditional) way to show their love and admiration—a modern man's way of acknowledging his awesome modern mate.

Though De Beers did not have a name for what it was doing at the time, the key to the success of the right-hand ring was story-doing: it identified that the metastory shared by millions of women had changed and that there were aspects of that story going unexpressed. The company designed a product that had that new story baked into it, introduced that story in a way that encouraged women to tell it to each other, and advertised only as necessary. This process led not only to success for the right-hand ring but to a series of successful launches, each one driving at least $1 billion and, in several cases, multibillion-dollar sales gains for De Beers. Two additional examples:

- *The three-stone anniversary ring:* To celebrate your past, your present, and your future.

- *Journey diamond jewelry:* With every step, love grows.

Each one of these launches followed the same pattern: discover an unarticulated story that men or women needed to express. Create a physical design for the jewelry that expressed that story. So for three stones, the unexpressed story went like this: "We have been married for some time now, long enough to have weathered a few storms. And I love you more today than when we first married. I can't wait for the next ten or twenty years." The physical expression of that story: the three-stone anniversary ring, one large diamond flanked by two smaller diamonds, each stone a symbol of a stage of your relationship, your past, your present, and your future.

For Journey diamonds, the unexpressed story went something like this: "Every relationship is a journey. We've been through our share of ups and downs and twists and turns, and what I have discovered is that over time, our love has deepened." The physical expression of that story was a jewelry design that always incorporated a series of stones arranged in ascending size—smaller to larger.

By understanding the story that needed to be expressed first, and then building that story into the product designs themselves, De Beers were making it much easier for the story to be understood by both the buyer (usually a man) and the recipient (usually a woman). They were creating products that came preloaded with all-important meaning.

The Four Truths

Subway and De Beers are examples of companies that grew up in the age of storytelling. They adopted some of the storydoing behaviors and processes that are becoming more and more widespread today and will become absolutely necessary for all businesses to

FIGURE 2-3

The metastory quad

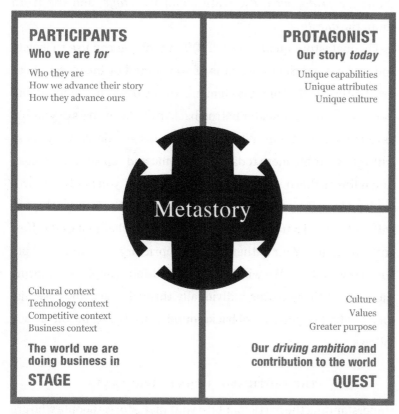

PARTICIPANTS
Who we are *for*

Who they are
How we advance their story
How they advance ours

PROTAGONIST
Our story *today*

Unique capabilities
Unique attributes
Unique culture

Metastory

Cultural context
Technology context
Competitive context
Business context

**The world we are
doing business in**

STAGE

Culture
Values
Greater purpose

**Our *driving ambition* and
contribution to the world**

QUEST

Metastory: What we wish to *become*
The narrative that will drive all the actions we take as a business.

thrive in the future. These behaviors and processes can be applied to any business of any size, from the coffee shop on the corner to the largest multinational corporation. But to understand them and put them to work in your business, you need a system to break the problem down into bite-size pieces. For your business to begin to engage in storydoing, there are *four key truths* that you need to explore and understand: the truth about the *participants,* the truth about the *protagonist,* the truth about the *stage,* and the truth about the *quest.*

The metastory quad (figure 2-3) is a tool you can use to isolate and understand the four truths of your brand or business. These four truths are the timeless elements to any powerful, moving, and motivating story; a theater patron back in Shakespeare's day would have recognized them. What the tool helps you do is apply these truths to your business today in a rational and repeatable process. And it forces thorough and holistic thinking. As you apply this process and learn to look at your business through the four truths, you will understand a tremendous amount about what makes it different and unique. Your authentic and proprietary metastory will begin to reveal itself. We will spend the next four chapters exploring each one of these truths individually through a specific case history, but to give you a bit of background, a brief description of each follows.

THE TRUTH ABOUT THE PARTICIPANTS

Understanding the participants in your metastory—people who are affected by or use your product or service—is the core of this truth. Your goal is to achieve a deep understanding of their motivations: what story are they telling with their lives and how can your story help them to do their story better? You can do this in a variety of ways (chapter 3 goes into this in detail), but the most important thing to remember here is that you shouldn't expect people to blurt out and announce their story. Although you might interview them (you should, in fact), you will learn the *real* truth about their story by observing what they do and the actions they take, rather than listening to what they say.

THE TRUTH ABOUT THE PROTAGONIST

This is the truth about your company and your business situation today. Since you have a vested interest here, it is important to be truly honest and self-critical when you consider this truth. Talk to people in your company. What are your strengths? Weaknesses? Where are you vulnerable to competitors? Where do you have real advantage? It helps to inventory a series of recent actions: an ad you ran, a company you bought, a product you launched, a person you hired or fired. When you string together all these actions you are taking as a company, do they seem consistent? What is the bigger story you are telling? It may seem odd to try to create a coherent narrative from a series of disconnected events. But your participants will be doing just that. To understand your story from their point of view, it is important to spend time talking with some of your participants. It is also important to talk to some people who have rejected your story and embraced a competitor, for whatever reason. These folks will tell you the truth about yourself (ready or not) and give you invaluable insight into opportunities to do your story differently in the future.

THE TRUTH ABOUT THE STAGE

This is the broader business and cultural stage on which your story is playing out. You want to examine four subaspects of the stage—economic, technological, cultural, and competitive. As you dig into each of these areas, look for handholds and footholds for your own competitive advantage. But more importantly, step back and look for larger cultural narratives playing out around you that will affect the way your story is perceived. Stories change over time, and paying attention to this can be life or death for your business. An example of almost constant cultural change is the story of wealth and, by extension, of luxury and luxury brands. The story of wealth used to be told through conscious display—massive homes filled with dark wood; precious metals; large, powerful automobiles; and exclusive club memberships. Today that story still exists, but a new story, "stealth-wealth," has arisen. This story is more about discretion and nondisplay. The average billionaire today is as likely to walk around her solar- or wind-powered home in jeans and a T-shirt as she is to drive the halls of her castle in her Bugatti Veyron. Paying attention to these shifts and the meaning behind them is vital.

THE TRUTH ABOUT THE QUEST

Last but not least is the truth about your quest. While the rest of these truths can be explored in any order—or simultaneously—this always comes last. Your quest is the aspirational mission of your company, brand, or product beyond making money. It is the higher ideal or human goal you have as a business. Red Bull doesn't want to only sell you cans of energy drink, it wants to "give you wings," which is the external tagline that encapsulates its quest to inspire you to push yourself hard in everything you do. HINT Water's quest is to take on the forces of big sugar and convince people to drink more water and less soda. Virgin's quest is to put some naughty fun back into the drab, dowdy businesses it invades: airlines, mobile phones, insurance. Companies with quests have a cause that transcends pure profit. It is a cause their participants can feel in all of their actions. The quest, more than any of the other truths, is the source of loyalty and fanaticism among your participants. As a result, companies with a clear and powerful quest have an almost unfair advantage over their competitors.

METASTORY

The four truths are the pillars of your metastory. Your metastory, as I've noted, is fundamentally what you want to *become* as a business. It has its roots planted firmly in the reality of your business today, but it is meant to be both aspirational and directive. You will see that the metastory examples in this book all end with the words "To do this, we will . . ." That's to ensure that as you shape the language in your metastory, it is directive—it leads to *action*. If those words don't feel right at the end of your metastory, it's a good bet you're not finished crafting it.

To articulate your metastory, you must first understand and have conviction around each one of the four truths. To help give you deeper insight into each one of them, and how they are discovered, we're going to spend the next four chapters diving more deeply into each one in turn through a specific case history. Then, in chapter 7 we will explore the process for synthesizing what you have learned into your own metastory, and, using a case to illustrate it, we will explore how to create an action map—the set of action principles that you will use to guide future actions for your company.

A few notes about these case histories: if you engage in this work yourself, you will often find that one of the four truths contributes disproportionately to the final metastory. These cases were chosen for that reason. All four truths are a part of each case, but I will emphasize the process used to discover the truth that made the greatest contribution to the final metastory. At the end of each chapter you will see how all four truths work together and how the final metastory quad looked when it was completely filled out for the case. So, while each chapter is devoted to a single truth, each will also add to your understanding of how the whole process works and how it all comes together at the end.

The cases cover a range of business situations, both larger and smaller companies, from a three-person start-up to a large global retailer to the launch of a new division for a big multinational. However, because all companies are unique, no one case will ever perfectly align to your situation. While each case contains material that you will find useful and relevant, there may be a specific aspect that makes it very different from your situation. Because of that, there is a section at the end of each case where we delve into the general principles that most companies would need to go through to get at each one of the truths for themselves. By interpolating between the specific cases and the general steps at the end, you should be able to apply the process to your own situation and your own company.

CHAPTER 3

The Participants

*A*udience is a word you still hear a lot in marketing, but it's an outdated term because the people experiencing a modern metastory are not passive observers. Your customers are emotional, and in many cases, physical *participants* in your metastory (figure 3-1).

But there are participants beyond your customers to consider as well. Your employees are important participants in your story. And many businesses have complex relationships with external partners who should also be considered participants: real estate, insurance, and financial services are businesses where external agents play a key role. Certainly, they should be considered participants as well. An imperative today is creating a story with which they all actually want to get involved—a story that helps them to actually do part of their personal metastory. This is the place where a lot of modern marketing falls apart. We are clear on our business goals. We take the time to get really smart about what's going on in the

FIGURE 3-1

The metastory quad: participants

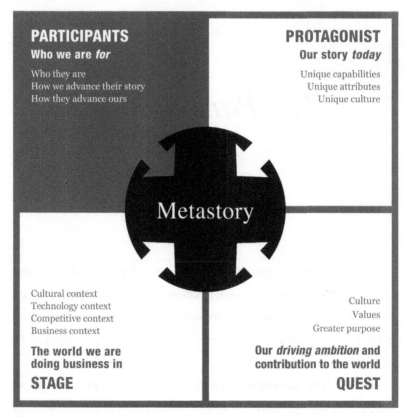

PARTICIPANTS
Who we are *for*

Who they are
How we advance their story
How they advance ours

PROTAGONIST
Our story *today*

Unique capabilities
Unique attributes
Unique culture

Metastory

Cultural context
Technology context
Competitive context
Business context

**The world we are
doing business in**

STAGE

Culture
Values
Greater purpose

**Our *driving ambition* and
contribution to the world**

QUEST

Metastory: What we wish to *become*
The narrative that will drive all the actions we take as a business.

world, culturally, technologically, and competitively. But instead of doing the work of really understanding our participants, finding out who they are and what story they are trying to tell with their lives, we define them as an audience, turn on the paid-media spigots, and push our often unwelcome and self-centered messages into their lives: *"Buy the Flamingo Polisher 3000 Today!!!"* $20 million

58

or $50 million or $100 million later, we sit back and wonder why it didn't work. Only by truly understanding your participants and the nuanced story they are trying to tell in their lives can you hope to tell your story in a way that will truly inspire them to participate. People are not simple creatures, and their authentic thoughts and feelings are not something they will blurt out in a focus group. I'll tell you I'm a mom in a focus group—I won't tell you I also see myself as a sexy and attractive woman. It is essential to find their real meta-story. Until we know that, we can't know how to tell *your* story.

A global retailer, which I'll call Stylebox, provides a perfect case example.

Runaway Brand Creation at Stylebox

Stylebox is known for making great design and high style available to the masses at very reasonable prices. Today there are over one thousand of these stores across the United States, from Miami to Seattle. Their brand is optimistic, modern, and a little cheeky.

Like many big-box retailers, this company features a huge number of famous national brands in its stores. But it also sells many of its own house brands. In early 2006, there was a growing suspicion that there might be too many house brands in the system. In its advertising, Stylebox was *telling* a very stylish and modern story, but by cluttering the store with irrelevant or unnecessary SKUs, it was *doing* a very different story. This dissonance was becoming noticeable to customers. It was degrading the experience they had with the stores, which wasn't good for the brand, short term. Longer term, it threatened the growth of the business by making it harder to scale. Each new product added friction to the system, and over time it could slow the whole business down. The senior vice president of marketing, then a thirty-three-year veteran of the company, was convinced that the house brands were a big part of the problem. She felt that they were actually confusing the stores' participants. She set out to first confirm the hunch and then to solve the problem—to make sure the participant experience in the store reflected the simplicity and stylishness so central to the company's metastory.

Within the branding business, this kind of job is known as framing a company's *brand architecture*—a term of art that defines which brands are needed, how they work together, and what story they jointly tell together. Of particular interest were questions like: How many house brands do we need? Which brands should cover which kinds of product? How similar or different should they look? What do they *do* for participants? How do they help the participants advance their own metastory?

To begin to answer these questions, a team from the marketing department visited a store to find and photograph all of the house brands "in the wild," as it were. The consensus in advance was that there were maybe seventy-five house brands. Days later, after scouring every corner of an understanding and very patient location in New Jersey, the team had found a shocking total of 225 brands. They had to create a sixty-foot long scroll in a corridor just to lay out all the names, logos, and photos of the packages for all the brands audited. This discovery resoundingly confirmed the original hypothesis, but it also led to new questions: Why so many? Where had they all come from? Had these house brands somehow evolved the ability to breed? The team assumed they would find the answers in the office of the person in charge of the house brands.

Tellingly, it took a little while to figure out exactly who that was. This particular company is made up of three separate and powerful management groups. The store operations group is made up of people who run the outlets, keep the employees happy, and manage the logistics to get the products to the store. But while store operations controlled aspects of the experience participants had in the store, they had no say in which brands should be where. There was a marketing group that ran the overall brand, including all of the advertising and promotions. But they weren't authorized to add or remove house brands; their job was to promote them. Last, there was the merchant group, which chose the products, bought them, and figured out how much to charge for them. It made sense to the team when they discovered that it was the merchant group that was in charge of the house brands. What surprised them, though, was that there was no centralized plan for the house brands, and no one person actually responsible for them.

In this organization, individual merchants each ran a separate silo of merchandise in the system. As in any retail business, there was massive pressure on the individual merchants to move the numbers upward in their category in a hurry. It turns out that an effective way for an individual merchant to do this is to create a new house brand, for two reasons. First, the company makes more money on its house brands than it does on national brands. Since the margins are higher, adding a new brand can quickly boost the margins in whatever category that merchant runs. Second, it's easier and quicker to create new brands now than ever before, because a responsive and high-quality manufacturing base has grown up in China and elsewhere. A new brand can be turned around in a matter of months: some phone calls to the company's sourcing operation, a request to marketing to create a logo, a high-level financial plan, and the brand is pretty much good to go. So the merchants— the people who "invented" the goods—had every reason to want to make new house brands. Meanwhile the marketers—the people who promoted the goods—weren't acting as a check on that behavior. Marketing people called merchants, in quotes, "the client," and their culture was to help the client achieve its goals, house-brand creation included. There was no one in the organization specifically tasked with understanding the overall story being told to participants through the experience in the store.

So the company turned out to be a huge house-brand-creation machine without an off switch. When you consider that a diverse group of merchants had created 225 different brands with no central plan, it isn't really all that surprising that some questionable choices were discovered. There was an entire brand called something like "Decorative Metal Animals," for instance. That was the name for a range of—don't hurt yourself trying to guess—decorative metal animals.

These metal animals bring up a few issues. First, an SKU, or even a group of them, isn't a brand. Just because you have a logo for decorative metal animals doesn't mean it deserves to be called a brand. A brand is a stable symbol for a set of reliable attributes that are familiar and predictable. Real brands come from somewhere. They have a story. Without a story, they have no meaning— they are useless at helping a participant advance her own story. The company was blizzarding participants with SKUs that had no story. They weren't brands so much as they were transactional tactics, and participants saw them as hollow. And there were way too many of them, so many that not even the marketers and merchants could keep track, let alone a harried thirtysomething mom with three kids hoping for a good deal that would also make her feel good about the choices she was making for her family. Her experience of the situation was actually the most important one, and unfortunately, it was becoming increasingly fragmented and confusing.

The way forward, then, was to put the *participant*, not the merchants, in charge of the house brands: to build the brand architecture around her. So the team set about understanding her in real detail.

Researching the Participants

The approach used by Stylebox is a good model for how to understand your participants because it was very deep but also comprehensively broad. The work involved five separate kinds of analysis, two specialist-research companies, and an extensive collaboration with an indefatigable in-store team who created new accounting codes and bought a spanking new server to house all the data.

They started with a straightforward analysis of Stylebox demographics. Of the stores' participants, 80 percent were women. And these women worked hard. On average, they were about thirty-three years old, with two kids. They usually had a full- or part-time job and then came home to take care of the house and the kids. Their husbands also worked. Their total household income was $40,000 to $50,000 a year, but they aspired to give themselves and their kids a better life. They were optimists at heart; that's why they chose to shop here rather than at other chains that were known for low prices but had no sense of style. These were smart, resourceful, and positive people. But the team had to dig deeper to really understand their motivations, the metastory they were telling through the choices they made inside the store.

First, the team ran a cluster analysis on what products participants put in their shopping carts and then purchased. The aim of a cluster analysis is to understand how and why certain products "cluster" together—why participants buy certain products along with other products in a predictable pattern. The aim is to use that knowledge as a foundation for understanding the role of the individual products in the overall story being told in the store. Think of a cluster as a chapter in a larger story. The larger story might be "I'm a good mom," and one chapter might be "I send my kids to school with a healthy brown-bag lunch every day." So one cluster might include peanut butter, jelly, whole wheat bread, apples, and organic juice boxes. Ideally, a new house brand should augment or round out a coherent cluster.

To do this work, the team actually had to buy a new, more powerful server because the volume of data overwhelmed Stylebox's largest computer at the time. They worked with the financial team to code the 225 house brands' financials to find out which ones participants were spending the most money on. They worked with a research firm to poll guests to find out who had heard of these house brands and, if so, what they thought of them. They tapped an ethnographic research firm to film a study of sixteen typical participants to understand their deepest motivations. And they went into the store, bought the products themselves, took them home, and used them in their daily lives.

What came through from every angle and every data run was that the guests felt overwhelmed. They loved the overall Stylebox brand with a passion, but they didn't like the house brands. For years, the company's advertising had painted a picture of a clean, modern, simple, gorgeous way of living, where happy young people move through a world of beautifully curated, useful objects. But actual visits to one of the stores had become a very different experience. Guests experienced overload—a cacophony of colors, words, and temptations yelling at them from the shelves. And that included too many house brands. The company was *telling* one story with its advertising, but *doing* the opposite story with these 225 brands. As a result, participants were only buying or recommending a few of them with any enthusiasm. Most people were unaware of the house brands even when prompted, and only a third of participants who were aware of the brands knew they were owned by the parent brand.

The recommendation: fewer, bigger, better house brands, handled in a way that told the overall brand story and actually helped guests navigate the store. The team worked on building a new house-brand structure, tailor-made for the participants. The new architecture included just thirty-five brands, each with a clear role and built on an actual cluster of purchasing. Decorative Metal Animals, to the dismay of almost no one, was slated for retirement. In a meeting of the merchandising and marketing teams, the chief merchant and the chief marketing officer made a blood vow to create no new brands and to reduce the complexity. A plan was created to change the management oversight of house brands, to assign a governing body to them, and to hire brand managers to run them. The company had begun the job of restructuring itself for storydoing.

A Generic Line in Need of a Nongeneric Story

As the team worked on the final house-brand architecture, sorting out real brands from shouldn't-be brands, they realized there was a very big part of the store that had a different problem. The "consumables" department in this company carries pretty much anything you might need for your daily life that isn't food, booze, or transportation. It rolls confidently from garbage bags, food storage, toilet paper, and detergent through hand sanitizer, deodorant, and shampoo and on to painkillers, antacids, and peroxide, stopping along the way at adult diapers, diet shakes, and fungal foot cream. This single department was home to everything you might find in an entire drugstore. It was home turf for the most storied marketers in the business, Procter & Gamble and Unilever, and some of their biggest brands: Crest, Gillette, Pampers, Tide, Dove, Axe, and Vaseline.

Within this behemoth department, the company had, like most large retailers today, created a generic line of products that provided similar functionality to some of the national brands, but underpriced those brands by an average of 30 percent. The generic brand was a bit of a chameleon, if not an outright lamprey. The generic brand's approach was to adopt a color scheme similar to that of a national brand (different enough to pass legal muster, of course) and put the company logo on it. For instance, the mouthwash package would be yellow and khaki, and the label might say "Alternative to Listerine." If it were next to Cascade dish-washing powder, it might be a green box with red and yellow lettering, and small letters would say something like, "Alternative to Cascade." Since this internal generic brand had no official name, some employees just called it something like "Alt and Save."

It turned out that there were a huge number of items under the Alt and Save brand—about 750 throughout the department. This led to some odd outcomes; for instance, the Alt and Save ibuprofen that sat next to the Advil wearing Advil-like packaging said, "Alternative to Advil," and the Alt and Save ibuprofen that sat next to Motrin wearing Motrin-like packaging said, "Alternative to Motrin." They were the exact same medical formulation—the exact same product. So in some cases Alt and Save was actually competing with *itself*. Suffice to say that some of the national brands were not thrilled with this state of affairs. The tense relationship and spirited legal wrangling between the national-brand sellers and the generic labels offered by major national retailers goes back many decades. And in a surprise twist, in some cases, a national brand ends up actually supplying Alt and Save with its own product—weird, but true.

LOOKING AT THE PROBLEM THROUGH THE EYES OF THE PARTICIPANTS

Most importantly, in this ongoing battle, it turned out that the people really getting beaten up were the participants, for a few reasons. First, since the generic brand had the famous and iconic retailer's logo on it but no name, people didn't know what to call it. In the ethnographic research, they'd call it "that one" or "this one" or "those over there." They'd say, "Well, there's Cascade, and I like that, and then there's 'that one' over there." It didn't really have a name. Remember when the musician Prince dropped his name for a few years and just used a symbol? It was kind of like that (though about a thousand times less interesting).

The second thing is that the brand often adopted the color scheme of the national brand it sat next to on the shelf. Thus, would-be house-brand loyalists had a difficult time finding it in a crowded store, even when they knew they wanted it. So a hard shopping trip was made even harder for a participant.

The third problem was a worrying perception of the generic brand's story by the participants. The ethnographic research firm that had been brought on had done a web survey asking about two thousand people what they thought of various brands in the store. People taking this survey clicked on the set of words that they most associated with a particular brand, choosing words for the overall brand and all the internal house brands. While participants loved the main brand and associated it with characteristics like "smart," "fresh," and "convenient" (exactly the kind of descriptors that the company hoped for), the characteristics they associated with Alt and Save were "value priced" and "practical." What this meant was that every purchase of Alt and Save was contradicting the overall metastory that the company was trying to tell. Alt and Save was dragging the main brand down.

The nail in the coffin came from the ethnographic research. The company went to great lengths to find out how people felt about the Alt and Save products in their homes. They gathered detailed information about how these people lived, what products they liked, and how they used them: how much dish soap they used on the dinner dishes, and where they kept the bottle; what kind of shampoo they preferred; how often they used mouthwash—the real details of how the story of the products and the story of the participants intermingled.

To accomplish this, the ethnographers and a small film crew team actually moved in with participants. They picked sixteen to study and spent about a day and a half with each. The film crew visited their houses, shopped with them, and interviewed each family member about their shopping experience. And they spent hours acting as flies on the wall, just observing the family. They would follow the family silently during a shopping trip, videotaping everything. Then they'd retrace the subject's steps, discussing the experience and getting a voice-over on the decision-making process.

The team learned that people loved the overall brand. They had some of the highest feelings of empathy and positivity toward the Stylebox brand that anyone on the team had ever seen. But when the subjects shopped at the store, they started to feel unsure and confused. When they compared products—especially between Alt and Save and the national brands—they didn't feel they were getting useful information. They didn't know what to call Alt and Save, and they thought it was really hard to locate it on the crowded shelves. It was like the main brand was dressing in drag. There was a disturbing 5 o'clock shadow.

From the participants' perspective, the experience overall ran completely counter to what the company might hope for. The products were hard to find, and when found, they said, "I'm an alternative version of the thing you can't afford." Because they could be interpreted as looking similar to the national brands, price became the only meaningful difference. The unintended effect was that participants who had to make that choice felt confronted by their own inability to afford the real thing. The story of the Alt and Save brand went something like this: "I might work as well as Brand X, and Brand X is really good, but, you know, I'm not really Brand X. I'm Brand X that's cheaper. Kind of like you." The emotional experience for guests was an unwelcome reminder of their inability to afford a good life, as defined by the famous national brands. Worse, since anyone who came into their homes would see this and immediately know what it meant, participants tended to hide it. That was sad, and it was unnecessary.

TAKING ACTION TO DESIGN THE EXPERIENCE
AROUND THE PARTICIPANTS

It was a classic metastory problem, and the team arrived at a story-led solution. The recommendation was to kill off Alt and Save and replace it with an entirely new "generic" brand with an entirely new metastory. It would be a metastory built around the needs of the most value-conscious participants. It would have its own clearly defined visual personality that would stand out proudly on the store shelves. It would be a brand that a single working mother, a woman with limited resources but big aspirations, would be proud to have in her home when friends and family dropped by. It was designed from the beginning to be a story that would inspire both loyalty and pride in the participants, a story that empowered participants to express something meaningful and positive about themselves by buying it and displaying it in their homes—and a story that didn't need to be told, or even supported by a big TV budget.

While this recommendation emerged naturally from a thorough investigation, it was not an easy sell. From the merchants' point of view, the team was proposing the removal of one of the best-loved American marks, the company's iconic logo—an all-star veteran if ever there was one—from over $1 billion worth of merchandise and replacing it with an untested rookie. The merchants had a lot to lose in this situation. But they also had a lot to gain if it went well. Some intense discussion and debate led to agreement: to create an alternative, but to test it carefully against the existing brand to be sure it would work before it saw broad application.

The questions then became: What values and personalities should this new brand have? What should it stand for? What the ethnographic research had clearly revealed was that the participants' experience of the current Alt and Save metastory was one of disappointment and economic pressure. It started with frustration and ended with a tiny sense of loss. It amplified any feeling they might have that they were losing in the world. It made everyday life a moment of negativity, of the inability to afford a good life for themselves and their families.

To change that, the team encouraged the company to instead offer a positive, affirming story through the new generic brand. The story needed to be one of optimism—participants should be given the chance to be optimistic in everyday, little moments in their lives. That became the central part of the metastory and helped the team create a brand that was about great stuff at a good value—*everyone* deserves to live a clean, stylish life.

The team spent a long time trying to name the new brand. This was a daunting task. They needed something that would speak to the participants and be easily identifiable. But they also had to come up with one that hadn't already been trademarked by someone else in any one of the forty-four product categories across the division, a division in which some of the biggest and smartest packaged goods companies—Procter & Gamble, Unilever, and so on—had been naming many, many products for a very long time. After a long and difficult process that invented and then rejected over a thousand names, they ended up with a name with an upbeat feeling and spoke to aspiration. We'll refer to it here as "Optimism" by Stylebox.

Once the name was agreed and vetted legally, a design was needed. From the start, it was clear that the brand's packaging should do the opposite of imitating the national brands: it should be a completely separate, distinct brand to which the participants could relate. In the end, they centered on a simple solution: a white background, with clear lettering, that was as straightforward as possible while still retaining a Swiss elegance. A big, optimistic symbol lives on the front label of each product, scaled to be visible at sixty feet so that guests can find it easily. At ten feet, guests can identify the product itself, since the type is clear and the first line of copy indicates the product name, not the brand. It's all about giving the participants the information they need to make their purchase easily while retaining a sense of humanity about the process. The lettering and the symbol can be any color that the merchant wants, as long as it's *not* the color of the most similar national brand. That was the only restriction the team placed on the packaging.

The result: a new shopping system, more than a packaging design. The brand acts as a helpful signpost throughout the store, constantly aiding guests as they locate it, narrow down their selection, compare what's on offer, and decide to buy.

Marketing was keen to go ahead. But some of the merchants were understandably terrified. There was a huge debate within the company about whether this would work. But with the rigor of the research and design, and with vocal support of the head merchant for consumables, the case was gradually won. Mockups of the packages were created for eyeball-tracking studies to see how well the new designs worked to attract customers' eyes. And, wow, did they work. That was actually a relief to the team, who were worried that the Swiss-modernist nature of the packaging might not be enough to compete in a test environment with all the crazy-pattern brands screaming holographically from the aisles. The new brand was designed to take that feeling away. The team was delighted when they saw that the new packages offered an island of calm in the chaos *and* attracted the eye by doing that.

The team wanted the brand to speak with intimacy and humanity and gentleness that made people feel comfortable and proud of what they were purchasing and using. They waited with bated breath and crossed fingers for the results.

Results and Conclusions

The proof came when the participants voted with their wallets. Upon launch, in the spring of 2009, the company saw revenues go up by 20 percent when a product was shifted from Alt and Save to

FIGURE 3-2

Stylebox metastory quad

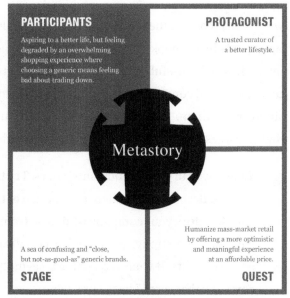

PARTICIPANTS

The insight that led to the "Optimism" metastory came from a comprehensive understanding of the Truth about the Participants.

Aspiring to a better life, but feeling degraded by an overwhelming shopping experience where choosing a generic means feeling bad about trading down.

PROTAGONIST

A trusted curator of a better lifestyle.

Metastory

A sea of confusing and "close, but not-as-good-as" generic brands.

Humanize mass-market retail by offering a more optimistic and meaningful experience at an affordable price.

STAGE

QUEST

Metastory: We will help "Stylebox's" most value-conscious Participants tell an optimistic story with the everyday products they need but have a hard time affording. "Optimism" will be the physical manifestation of their everyday optimism. To do this we will:

the new brand (figure 3-2). These results gave the company the confidence to grow the range further, taking it from 740 items to around a thousand today and expanding it into new areas such as stationery.

In addition to creating a successful line of generics, the new brand has had an impact on the company's brand. It actively advances the Stylebox metastory in ways that Alt and Save never could. What the team is most proud of, though, is that the participants have an option that's all about the upside, not about trading down, and that was built for them and being grown by them.

Five Things You Need to Do to Discover the Truth about *Your* Participants

For obvious reasons, there won't be a lot you can learn about your participants in any book or magazine. Their personal blogs and social media can be useful. But fundamentally, the truth about your participants will come from going out among them, spending time talking with them, living with them, videotaping them—doing whatever it takes to really become intimate with their lives.

1. Take a walk in your participants' shoes. Try their lives on for size. Become one of them for a period of time. Experience the story your company is "doing" from their point of view. Look for strengths, but look especially for weaknesses or disconnects. If your advertising is saying "We're the company that cares," but your customer service people are rude or seem to be in a real hurry to get participants off the phone, that's a problem. Go buy some of your own products. Load up on your company's shampoo and body wash, and see what the experience of buying it and using it is like. Eat your own frozen chicken patties, drive on your own tires, wear your own skinny jeans. If your skinny jeans are, you know, *skinny*, call your own customer service and ask them how to loosen them up. When customer service tells you that, they are really sorry, but skinny jeans are *meant* to be skinny, debate that idea with them to get a feel for what a participant experiences when he or she puts pressure on your system. Order something online and unpack it in your home. Are there annoying foam peanuts everywhere? Make

a note to yourself to ditch the annoying foam peanuts. By experiencing your business through the eyes and ears of your participants, you can start to really feel your metastory—not the story you think you're doing or you hope to do, but the story you are actually doing in the world today. The real deal. This knowledge sets you up to understand what you might need to do differently in the future.

2. Live with your participants if you can. Visit them in their homes, watch how they live and work and play. Capture this experience, either on video or in detailed notes. An in-depth professional ethnography study can be incredibly helpful to understand more about your participants. Companies can be brought in to do extremely deep dives into how your participants are living and working today. If you can't afford that level of discovery (they are a premium product), there is a lot you can do all on your own. Bring your own product to participants' homes and videotape them as they use it. This will feel awkward at first. Do it. You'll get used to it, and so will they. Follow them on a shopping trip. Spend a few days in their homes, experiencing life as they live it. You will find that many participants actually enjoy these visits, because it's one of the rare times they experience a company actually listening to them. And the insights you gather here can be invaluable.

3. Often people won't tell you what they really think in a focus group. If you can't get to a really comprehensive ethnography, at the very least interview a few people in one-on-ones. People won't tell you their real motivations in a group

setting, but when you talk to them as individuals, you may be able to probe into their hopes and dreams for themselves and for their families.

4 Use these real experiences and real stories from your participants to build detailed personas. Resist stereotypes and generalities when thinking about the true story they are trying to tell. It is very easy to fall into deeply unhelpful demographic clumps: "At Acme Sausage, we target women eighteen to forty-nine years old." Have you ever met a woman aged eighteen to forty-nine? You need to know that you are trying to help Kathy Jones, a twenty-six-year-old African American mother of three, tell her true story. She's a Pisces, likes spicy food, and goes skydiving on the weekends.

5 Remember, until you know the story Kathy is trying to tell with her life, you won't understand how to tell your own in a way that is useful to her. Gather data, experiences, and impressions to form a comprehensive understanding of how people are living with and using your product. The more you understand about who your participants really are, what their motivations are, what their hopes and dreams are, the better able you will be to figure out how your metastories will interact—how to do your story in a way that helps them to do theirs.

CHAPTER 4

The Protagonist

The truth about the protagonist homes in on the real truth about your business or brand today (see figure 4-1). All companies have strengths and weaknesses. What are yours? Are you an underfunded start-up struggling to poke through in a promising new market? Are you a hulking global colossus with plenty of resources but a risk-averse culture? Do you need to open up a new market? Have you been de-positioned by a competitor? What do your customers think about you right now? Are they rabidly loyal fanboys and fangirls, ready to jump to your defense if anyone criticizes you? Or are you a commodity, like air, noticeable mostly only if you were to disappear? And most importantly, where is your future growth going to come from?

As you explore the truth about the protagonist, it is important to dig hard and be honest with yourself about where your strengths lie and, more importantly, where you may be vulnerable. Business is a battle, and your competitors are going to look for every weakness

FIGURE 4-1

The metastory quad: protagonist

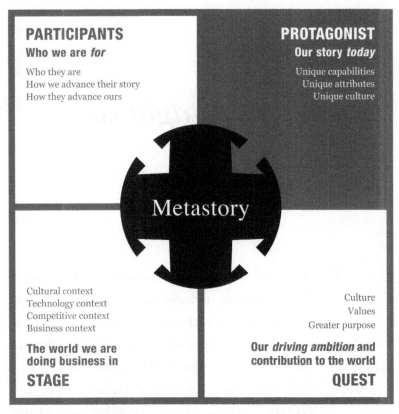

PARTICIPANTS
Who we are *for*

Who they are
How we advance their story
How they advance ours

PROTAGONIST
Our story *today*

Unique capabilities
Unique attributes
Unique culture

Metastory

Cultural context
Technology context
Competitive context
Business context

**The world we are
doing business in**
STAGE

Culture
Values
Greater purpose

**Our *driving ambition* and
contribution to the world**
QUEST

Metastory: What we wish to *become*
The narrative that will drive all the actions we take as a business.

they can exploit. Better to identify those weaknesses yourself and develop a plan for dealing with them before your competitors try to use them against you. The key is to find a way to look at the real truth about your brand or business that also maximizes your competitive advantage.

The protagonist is the hero of your story. But as in all stories, the protagonist doesn't play alone on the stage. There are often other major characters. For instance, the protagonist can be a new brand or business that is being launched by an *existing* business. In this case, there are actually two stories that you need to pay attention to: the story of the parent company, and the story of the new venture. The relationship between those two stories is important. If you are the person in charge of growing the new venture, you need to understand the narrative of the parent as clearly as you do the narrative of the new venture. That story can either help you or hurt you. This concept was particularly important when News Corporation set out to launch an ambitious new venture, a new digital-education division that came to be called Amplify.

News Corporation Enters the Education Business

In the spring of 2011, News Corporation was already a large and well-established global media company with a widely known story. Rupert Murdoch, the founder and CEO, was a legendary and some would say controversial figure on the global business scene. Ferociously smart and competitive, Murdoch had risen from relative obscurity in Australia to build a media empire that controlled over eight hundred companies in fifty countries, including dozens of newspapers, film studios, cable and satellite television companies, and a diverse set of publishing companies, sprawled across five continents. His overall business strategy appeared to be to identify a market or business that was hemmed in by some traditional structure or constraint and to disrupt that market or business by introducing innovation. Along the way he had earned a reputation for being a hard-nosed businessman and a very tough negotiator, in particular by buying struggling newspapers in New York and London and returning them to profitability by breaking the backs of the printers' unions. At the age of eighty-one, showing no signs of even thinking about retiring, he was charging ahead with his next audacious mission—to transform the nature of public education globally.

Murdoch had spoken publicly for several years about the appalling state of education in the world, and particularly in the United States, where News Corporation is headquartered and where Murdoch is a naturalized citizen. He saw the US education system as frozen in time, a relic of a distant analog past that was ripe for disruption and innovation. He pointed out that if you compared a photo of a classroom in the early 1900s and a modern classroom, the only substantial difference would be the color of the chalkboard. What other industry could say that? Technology, and specifically digital technology, had rolled through and transformed industry after industry—entertainment, finance, health care, manufacturing, publishing, and retail. DC-7s have given way to Dreamliners. Telegrams have given way to the internet and smartphones. Yet the way teachers taught and kids learned remained as it was at the dawn of the Industrial Age. Today, digital connection and communication capabilities are table stakes in any industry you can name. Not so in education—it's as if innovation stopped with Thomas Edison, or maybe Henry Ford's assembly line. In the majority of schools, education is still a factory-based model, where both teachers and students are treated as interchangeable widgets to be plugged into and out of a standardized platform. Meanwhile, outside of our public schools, the whole world has changed, transformed by technology.

This chasm is especially apparent to a new generation of young, digitally native teachers who have grown up with technology embedded in their daily lives. They are shocked at the lack of it when they enter their classrooms for the first time.

Murdoch believed that digital technology had the ability to change this sorry state, that teaching and learning could be reimagined. Digital technology could enable individual teachers to specialize in the things they particularly loved or at which they excelled, and students could do the same while they pursued learning at a pace and in a time and place that best suited them. For example, a teacher who was knowledgeable and inspiring on the topic of the Civil War could lecture ten thousand kids at a time, not thirty. And a teacher who excelled at one-on-one encouragement in arithmetic could choose to concentrate on that. And wouldn't it be great if kids used software that "learned" as they did, changing the lesson plans to fit their learning styles? None of this was science fiction. This was all possible using readily available tools, if only they could be applied.

Innovation in education *was* occurring, but it was happening mostly outside of public schools. What little innovation there was generally took place in the wealthy suburban schools or online, with sites like Khan Academy. Bigger, poorer inner-city school systems were being left behind. This fact seemed to particularly offend Murdoch, a staunch believer in the conservative principle of self-determination, which holds that individuals all have to earn their own way in the world. But he also believes that everybody should start from the same place so it's a fair fight. He wanted a solution that could be applied directly to the largest and poorest school systems in the country. He was passionate about this vision, and believed it could change the lives of millions of kids—and, yes, turn a profit in the process.

AMBITIOUS GOALS

Murdoch's ambition for Amplify was vast and inspiring—to address the poor state of innovation in public education, not around the edges, but with a root-and-branch reimagination of the space. This would require a comprehensive and coordinated approach in three distinct areas: data, compelling interactive software curricula, and a mobile distribution platform to transform the whole system.

First, teachers needed better measurement tools. When complete, this *data* layer would allow teachers to visualize an entire curriculum and see immediately the status of each student in that curriculum. Teachers could see where the students were strong, where they needed development or personal attention, and what subjects they had not yet taken on. Introduced into schools at scale, this layer would free teachers from marching clumps of students through the same material at the same pace. It had the potential to allow teachers to focus on inspiration as well as individual attention. It would change the way students and teachers could connect and interact; teacher-student ratios of 1–30 could become 1–10,000 or 1–1 easily and in a scalable way.

The second area was curriculum. To date, the approaches being taken in the digital arena in curriculum were either to replicate the app market on iTunes by creating small, "snackable" knowledge nuggets or to digitize textbooks by adding video and allowing them to run on an iPad or a Kindle—the same soup served in a new bowl. The core management team at Amplify believed that a better approach was to create an immersive and interactive education experience made *specifically* to run on digital platforms so that it took full advantage of the new medium. They sought to bring the production levels of digital films like *Avatar* to the education space and allow students to explore and, as they say in gaming, "level up" as they went.

The third area was distribution. The new division believed that teaching and learning needed to break out of the constraints set by the clock and the physical walls of a school. To realize that vision, tablets were key. So the third part of the plan was to introduce a tablet with a user interface specifically designed for an education environment and education tools. This is where the whole stack came together. The teacher view on the tablet would allow teachers to track, assess, and provide feedback to kids easily. The student view would allow kids to see where they were in the curriculum and how they were doing. Kids who were struggling could meet with a teacher one-on-one for individual instruction. The system allowed for a much more student-centric model of education.

When you begin to understand the implications of the approach, you immediately realize that today, school can be conducted in a new way. Today students *go into* school to get lectured as a group on a subject—something easily achieved today from home through videoconference or through prerecorded videos on YouTube. They *leave* school to do homework—which is the time students are most likely to have questions and where individual attention from the teacher would be most beneficial. A whole new approach could free teachers from their "group-based" duties during big parts of their day to focus instead on working with individual students, answering specific questions. Students could spend other parts of their day or evening "attending" large-scale lectures for ten thousand or one hundred thousand students.

BIG CHALLENGES

Launching this new business was a complex assignment, to say the least. To get to the truth about the protagonist for this new division, the team had to learn about a number of things simultaneously. First, there was just a baseline need to understand the state of education in the United States, both historically and today. Even excluding private education, it was a massively complex space, involving federal, state, and local governments; large traditional public school systems; charter schools; teachers' unions; teachers; parents; and last—but certainly not least—kids.

The team also needed to understand the parent story of News Corporation, since Amplify would be funded by it. A complex, global business even on an average day, News Corporation had recently become embroiled in a scandal around the hacking of cell phones by executives in some of its UK-based newspaper subsidiaries. In addition to being a major distraction to the company's senior executives, the scandal made the News Corporation name radioactive in education circles.

There were other aspects of the News Corporation story that made the education space particularly challenging as well. One of them was right there in its name: *corporation.* In education circles, there was already a mistrust of corporations getting involved with schools. Opponents had given this trend the somewhat alarmist label of *privatization.* The antiprivatization argument was that corporations had no business educating our children. The truth is, corporations have been providing products and services for public schools for years in the form of textbooks, cafeteria services, furniture, AV equipment and materials, learning toys, games, playground equipment, and sports equipment. So understanding the origins and the real agenda behind this anticorporation argument would be important.

Another issue, more specific to News Corporation, was Murdoch's reputation as a union buster. Key participants like the teachers' unions questioned News Corporation's real agenda in education and wondered if Murdoch was out to get *them* now, too.

Never one to waste time, Murdoch had already brought in Joel Klein, the former New York City schools chancellor under Mayor Michael Bloomberg, to run the new division. A fighter and a winner, Klein had gotten great results in New York in a very short time, and along the way made a few powerful enemies who were going to be factors in the outcome for the News Corporation education initiative. Klein quickly surrounded himself with a great core team of educators and innovators to get the new division off the ground. These included Kristen Kane, his former number two at the New York City schools; Diana Rhoten, a seasoned innovator and entrepreneur in the education space; and Peter Gorman, the former head of the Charlotte-Mecklenburg schools in North Carolina, a system that had made great strides under his guidance.

Murdoch had also made the first of several planned acquisitions in the education space, buying a thriving education-software company called Wireless Generation. So yet another important role for the protagonist and the overall metastory was to ensure that the employees of Wireless Generation continued to feel excited and motivated as it transitioned from being an independent start-up to sitting at the core of a larger and more ambitious enterprise (and at the center of a PR firestorm as well). The acquisition also added two key players from the Wireless Generation team to the core team of the new division: founder and executive chairman Larry Berger and CEO Josh Reibel. For the time being, this star-chamber was operating under the unimaginative name of News Corporation Education Division.

The ambitions of this core team, while inspiring, would have been tough enough to realize if everything else were perfect, and things were far from perfect. Soon after purchasing Wireless Generation, the simmering phone-hacking scandal in the United Kingdom blew up into a global media circus. Reporters at the News Corporation–owned *News of the World* newspaper in London had previously been investigated for hacking into the voicemail of celebrities, royals, and politicians to get stories. Then, in 2011, they were alleged to have hacked into the voicemail of some victims of the July 7, 2005, London terrorist attack and relatives of deceased soldiers in order to get sensationalist scoops. But they went too far when they allegedly hacked into the voicemail of the family of a murdered schoolgirl and erased crucial messages, which had a devastating effect on the girl's family. Very quickly it became clear that the scandal wasn't just about a couple of rogue reporters; soon, the company's entire culture, including one of Murdoch's sons, a top deputy, and even Murdoch himself, was being investigated. Murdoch eventually admitted that some of his employees had staged a cover-up.

All of this was pretty shocking stuff to the six rock-star educators who'd just signed on with great hope to run an ambitious new education start-up. Diana Rhoten, the chief strategy officer of the new division, was in Human Resources going through her new-employee orientation when news of the scandal broke. She had been on the faculty of Stanford University; had cofounded Startl, a company that advised for-profit digital and education-technology start-ups; and had been a program director in cyber-infrastructure for the National Science Foundation. Hacking Gwyneth Paltrow's cell phone was the last thing on her mind, and the last thing with which she'd want to be associated.[1]

Following the initial unpleasant surprise, there were almost immediate commercial ramifications. Wireless Generation lost out on a contract with a major metropolitan school system, ostensibly because of its association with the scandal. This was a company that, until the recent acquisition, had been seen as the best in the business, with best-in-class products. The products certainly hadn't changed, nor had any of the people. But they were suddenly doing business in a whole new environment.

With shock also came resolve, however. The core team was a group of seasoned professionals who had signed up for what they had already known would be a very tough assignment. This new wrinkle was just another barrier to contend with. They knew that Murdoch and News Corporation truly believed in the ambition of the team. They knew this support would make a huge difference in the long run. Many people who had gone down this road before—attempting to change the deeply entrenched US educational system—had failed because of a lack of resources or patience. This was not a problem that would be fixed in six months or a year or two years or three years. This was a long-term endeavor that required a deep commitment of time, energy, and resources.

The question they faced was how to create a narrative for the new protagonist that would express this genuine intent; a narrative that would capture the genuine optimism and conviction to drive change; a narrative that didn't deny an association with News Corporation but that carried as little baggage as possible from the parent story along with it.

Researching the Protagonist

The discovery phase of this project was massive. The purpose was to clearly and proactively define a protagonist narrative for the new division that didn't hide from its association with parent News Corporation but that stated its own clear difference and purpose. This was critical to the success of the new division, because left to its own devices, the world was already creating its own, potentially negative story. The real drivers of this new protagonist narrative would be found through interviews with the internal senior teams in News Corporation to understand their real motivations. But first the team had to gain a more comprehensive understanding of the entire education space, including how News Corporation was perceived in it. This was accomplished through a combination of focus groups and desk research. (As you engage in this for your own company, remember, leave no stone unturned.)

DESK RESEARCH, MAGAZINES, BOOKS, WEBSITES, AND VIDEO

The protagonist would have some powerfully established competitors right out of the gate, so it was important to comprehensively map the competitive landscape. The team began by doing a mountain of reading and viewing, poring through the websites and marketing materials of over twenty-five potential competitors, including the traditional players like Pearson, Scholastic, McGraw-Hill, and Houghton Mifflin; the new school upstarts like Khan Academy, LeapFrog, and School of One; and some potentially very powerful outsiders who were also eyeballing the space, like Apple. It was clear that digital education was a vibrant field, with many different entities trying many different approaches. But the space was also potentially quite confusing, particularly to parents who might be trying to parse these approaches for their own child. And none of the approaches even came close to the depth and breadth of the ambition for News Corporation's new division.

The team dug into books and videos about teachers, parents, and kids: viewing fifty-plus videos on the Education Nation Teacher Wall; reading numerous school-related speeches by educators like Gary Smuts, superintendent of the ABC Unified District in California, and Mitchell Chester, commissioner of the Massachusetts Department of Early and Secondary Education; watching TED videos on education; reading editorials written by educators and parents; and poring through a variety of magazines and newsletters from the wonky (*Edweek*) to the mainstream (*Parenting*). The team scoured the websites of unions and professional and philanthropic organizations. They also dug through a pile of education-trend reports.[2]

The protagonist would be doing business in a very complex sector that was changing almost daily, so the team read everything that had been published recently on the topic of education in current mass media.[3]

They also read a dozen books about the subject, but by far the most useful resource for understanding the history of education and the reform movement, as well as the current lay of the land, was a book called *Class Warfare,* by Stephen Brill.[4] That book laid out some very worrying numbers detailing how little progress has been made in academic achievement despite huge increases in expenditures per student. The team learned just how old, entrenched, and rancorous the debate about education is, and how deeply drawn the battle lines are. Brill detailed the problem of tenure, championed by the teachers' unions, which today has created a huge voting block of older teachers with zero incentive to embrace change. Another Brill observation that became pivotal to the thinking on this project was that the terms of the debate between "reformers" and the teachers' unions had been framed as a zero-sum game: gain for kids *must* come at the expense of labor protections for teachers. This wasn't true, but it was passionately argued. No wonder the teachers were resistant.

The picture that emerged of the marketplace that the protagonist would be entering first—public education in the United States—was pretty dire. In 2011, for instance, a quarter of US high schoolers didn't graduate—which means the United States ranked twenty-first in the world in graduation rates.[5] Worse than that, only about half of African American and Latino students graduated on time.[6] And the dropout rates were staggering: in all, 1.3 million students dropped out of school every year; that's equivalent to the population of seven entire schools every day.[7] Of those who did graduate, over three-quarters were rated "unprepared" for college.[8] So it was no surprise that almost two-thirds of them didn't successfully graduate from college even if they managed to get there.[9]

There is a devastating cost to all of this—to individuals, to society, and to our economy. For instance, over 40 percent of recent high school dropouts don't have a job—compared with a just over 4 percent unemployment rate for people with a college degree.[10] A high school dropout earns $260,000 less than a high school graduate does over his or her lifetime.[11] The poverty rate for families headed by dropouts is more than twice that of families headed by high school graduates.[12]

Clearly, the system is badly broken. One refrain of reformers had been that policy makers needed to spend more money on the problem. But again, a hard look at the statistics threw that solution into question: real education spending per student has more than doubled over the last thirty years.[13] Yet results have remained flat. More money alone wasn't going to solve the problem.

Another widely held belief that the team at Amplify sought to prove or disprove was that there was low deployment of technology in education. That turned out to be depressingly true, despite the growth of teenagers using a variety of devices—from tablets to portable gaming systems—outside the classroom. There's one person per PC in the United States as a whole, but 5.3 students per PC in US classrooms.[14] And where there *is* technology, it isn't being used. Only 40 percent of teachers report using computers "often" in their classrooms even though there's clear evidence that if deployed well, it works: time spent on rich and creative uses of technology is correlated with higher test scores.[15] Of schools that have implemented one-to-one computing, 58 percent see fewer dropouts, and fully 81 percent of schools that are implementing one-to-one programs effectively are seeing lower dropouts.[16]

The result is that students are emerging from our current system of education completely unprepared for today's digital world: a gap has formed between the knowledge and skills students are acquiring in schools and the knowledge and skills needed to succeed in the increasingly global, technology-infused twenty-first-century workplace.[17] One statistic that got the team's attention was this: it was estimated that 65 percent of children entering grade school in 2012 will end up working in careers that haven't even been invented yet![18]

No one disagreed that the results were terrible, but there was lack of agreement on how to tackle the problem. There were plenty of discussions about it online and elsewhere. The team found a trove of videos showing gatherings of parents and teachers talking about what they needed out of education, as well as some compelling TV programs and documentaries focused on the issue. Films like *Race to Nowhere* and *Waiting for Superman* delved into the issues and potential solutions, but both emphasized the fact that to make meaningful progress, there were some very high barriers to climb.

FOCUS GROUPS AND TEACHER ETHNOGRAPHY

After all that reading, the team really wanted to get firsthand input to understand the various groups of people that the protagonist would have to appeal to. So a set of focus groups, comprising key participants like parents, teachers, and school administrators, was held. The experts at Glover Park, a well-known research company that has a thriving business in both the private and the government sectors, executed these. The goal was to get a mix of urban and suburban responses, so Chicago and Richmond (Virginia) were chosen, with multiple groups being conducted in each city. The topics probed were diverse but fell into three main buckets: the role of digital innovation in education, the value proposition for the new division's product offering, and an understanding of how the News Corporation story was perceived by these various groups.

All of the audiences responded positively to the idea of "a twenty-first-century digital-learning approach" as long as it wasn't served up instead of "the basics." They also liked when technology was discussed as an enhancer and as a supplement to the teacher, not as a replacement.

All the participants were drawn to an approach that engaged kids with gamelike characteristics and interactive content, and instruction that was individualized. Teachers felt it could make teaching more individualized, iterative, and interesting. The approach clearly needed to be less about making teaching more efficient and more about helping teachers become more productive—not just about saving time but making the best use of their time. They wanted something that could help them teach differently and better, not just compute grades or tabulate scores on standardized tests faster. Parents were attracted to the ability to be more involved and to have a better understanding of their child's learning process, not just receiving the grades on a piece of paper through the mail or e-mail. And administrators were excited about how quickly and readily the data on both teachers and students could be made available and how useful it could be for helping both teachers and students improve.

There was a surprisingly low awareness of the scandal. The team concluded that this didn't mean it was a nonissue. It just meant that it was less of a consumer issue at the time, and more of a potential media issue—a media issue that would rapidly become a consumer issue if not carefully managed.

During this process, the team also visited a number of schools around the country, spending whole days watching teachers at work. This experience was an eye-opener. They found that computers outside of the administration offices, if any, were often huddled together in a "lab" that the kids would visit a couple of times a week. Computers used in the classroom, if any, were old and stored on rolling carts that teachers had to share. Wi-Fi was spotty or nonexistent. In older schools, power outlets for running or charging devices were scarce. There was virtually no tech support. Teachers often relied on individual tech-savvy parents or friends to install new software or unlock a frozen screen. The wealthier the school district, the more digitally attuned it was. But in general, technology was an afterthought. The message was stark: the people really at risk were the kids from poorer families that didn't have laptops and iPads at home. It was clearly discriminatory, intentionally or not.

ONE-ON-ONE INTERVIEWS

With the foundation of the desk research and focus groups in place, the team felt ready to dig into the one-on-one interviews that would most directly inform the creation of the protagonist narrative. They started with Murdoch himself, proceeded through selected top management at News Corporation (HR, operations, PR), then to Klein and the core team in the new Education Division, including the top management team at Wireless Generation. They also spoke with a list of luminaries and experts in the field of education outside the company—school superintendents for several large, urban-school systems; entrepreneurs who were trying innovative new approaches in education; venture capitalists who were investing in education start-ups; futurists; even a former governor of Florida.

The team learned a huge amount from the outsiders, but the interviews that were really key to discovering the truth about the protagonist were the interviews with the people inside News Corporation, and specifically the top people from the Education Division. These were the people who would form the culture of the company and define the set of actions that would become the Amplify metastory. What were their real motivations for joining this enterprise? After all, these folks had all had thriving careers in the public and private sectors in education before joining this venture. Yet they had dropped what they were doing and come together to take on a very hard problem. *Why?*

An inspiring story emerged. While it was true that Amplify was a for-profit venture and had to return shareholder value, this factor was secondary when the division leaders talked about their personal motivations. This was true all the way up to the top. Murdoch talked about fairness. "It's for the kids," he said several times in the interview, becoming visibly emotional and pounding his hand on the table for emphasis.

Joel Klein talked about his childhood. He'd grown up in humble circumstances, in a housing project in Woodside, Queens, and would never forget the great teachers who told him not to let his family's poverty hold him back. They expected big things of him, and they certainly motivated him to deliver. First in government in Washington, DC (he was the lead litigator in the government's case against Microsoft), then as a lawyer in private practice and in business, and later as the New York City schools chancellor.

In that position, with over one million students under his watch, Klein had gained a reputation as a reformer who wasn't afraid of a fight. He revealed that his years at the helm in New York had convinced him that technology, if applied correctly, could help a school system reimagine its methods and transform the education of children. Both Klein and Murdoch talked about results.

"Digital innovation won't get us anywhere if the results don't get better. We believe in rigor, in measurement and getting better results. If we don't do that, nothing else we do will matter," Klein said. He also pointed out that in the United States, innovation happened most often in the private, not the public, sector. He had joined News Corporation because he felt that there was a fearlessness and a willingness to take risks that didn't exist in government. It was where he could do the most good for the most people.

These points were echoed over and over by other team members. Why had they joined? "Balls and money," said one. They saw News Corporation as fearless, not concerned with the status quo, and deep-pocketed. "Here the team can be a real agent of change because we're unencumbered by legacy interests," said another.

It also emerged that these people were fundamentally pro-teacher. There was a strong belief that this new company should add value to teachers' work and lives. The players were well aware that teachers in general felt threatened by currently popular education reforms, like performance-based pay and evaluations based on standardized testing. They felt that delivering value to teachers—by actually improving their ability to teach—was necessary

And then there was the elephant in the room: there was a strong feeling among all the team members that the new brand would have to separate itself from News Corporation, both to insulate the new division from the scandal and to foster a more entrepreneurial spirit.

IMPLICATIONS: A THIRD WAY

As the team began to analyze the results, it became clear that they would need to reconcile several potentially opposing narratives to find the truth about the protagonist.

First there was the story of News Corporation. The name commanded attention and respect, but it also clearly came with complications. The financial backing of News Corporation conveyed serious intent in the education space, something the new division would absolutely benefit from. However, the conservative political bent and the antiunion threads of the News Corporation story were real factors. The new Education Division wasn't anti-anything. It was pro-results. It had no desire to pick fights with unions. That needed to be clearly conveyed from the outset. And of course, there was the hacking scandal, a daily drip of publicity poison with an uncertain outcome. All of this led the team to the conclusion that the name "News Corporation Education Division" was not going to cut it. It aligned the protagonist story of the offspring too closely with the parent. A new name and new story were going to be necessary.

The second important story was that of Joel Klein. As the leader of the new division, his professional narrative was going to be a big factor in how this division was perceived. There was no one (not even enemies) who didn't respect Klein and what he had accomplished in his life; his personal story would have inspired Horatio Alger himself. But in the education space, Klein's story had become closely aligned with the education-reform movement. As the New York City schools chancellor, he had found himself on the opposite side of issue after issue with the teachers' unions as he overhauled one of the biggest school systems in the country. The battle had become heated at times, with both sides pulling no punches. But that was the past. As far as the new Education Division was concerned, reform was yesterday's fight. "Words like *reform* and *accountability* are words that should be used around prisons, not schools" was a quote from a team member. The protagonist's narrative for the new Education Division wasn't that of a crusading reformer out to take on the teachers' unions. The narrative was about partnering with anyone serious about fundamentally reimagining education for students, parents, and teachers. It needed to be made clear from the beginning that the new division was pro-teacher at its core. First, because the whole team, Klein included, fundamentally believed that they could help teachers have happier, more productive, and more fulfilling careers. But also, on a purely commercial basis, teachers had a lot of influence over what technology was purchased.

School chancellors wouldn't buy anything the teachers didn't want to use, so teacher endorsement was crucial.

The teachers' unions were another factor. In *Class Warfare*, Stephen Brill had laid out the history of the unions in great detail. In the beginning they had done a lot of good, ending rampant abuse of vulnerable and isolated teachers. Over the decades they had helped elevate pay, reduce workload, and make teaching a revered and attractive career option. But Brill argued that over time, as the world changed, as new technologies became available, the unions had lost touch with the real goal: better education for kids. It's easy to see how this happened. It comes down to simple arithmetic—the more teachers there were, the more dues-paying members the unions potentially had. Consequently, more, better-paid teachers had become their *raison d'être*. Those goals didn't necessarily include *better* teachers or *happier* teachers.

The unfortunate outcome, Brill argued, was that the unions often lobbied against change, or they argued for incremental change. They feared corporations getting involved in schools and bringing technology into schools because the potential "efficiency" that came with these innovations meant the possibility of fewer teachers in the future. So they created alarming buzzwords like *privatization* to suggest nefarious corporate goals. From the union perspective, digital technology in schools was something to be contained, not embraced. The bogeyman they raised up to teachers was of the autoworkers who had lost their jobs to robots on assembly lines.

In fairness, there were real questions about the efficacy of previous attempts to introduce digital technology into schools. Many promises had been made and broken by people evangelizing for the latest gadget or gizmo. So some caution was definitely warranted. However, an unfortunate side effect of the hard-line anti-innovation stance was that the unions, even with all good intentions, were preserving the factory system of education, one that frustrated great teachers as much as it did parents and students. Ironically, getting teachers off the assembly line and freeing them to actually inspire and teach more effectively was one of the potential promises of digital technology in education. Teaching is hard work on a *good* day. In the current system teachers spend a huge amount of time on drudgery, paperwork, and bureaucracy. The right technology could help that. This part of the protagonist narrative—that the new division wasn't antiunion *or* pro-reform but pro-teacher and pro-results—had to be thought through carefully. The unions would be either powerful allies or adversaries, with huge membership bases and real political muscle.

The school administrators, parents, and kids were caught in the middle of all this. They just wanted school to be more inspiring, and they wanted better results. The fact that kids were dropping out in record numbers was testament to the fact that the current system was a disaster. It was a tragedy and something that needed immediate attention. Not through a "digital Band-Aid," but through a comprehensive rethinking of the system. While the new division had no desire to pick a fight, it wouldn't be helpful to kowtow either.

As the team turned this dilemma over in their minds, conviction began to form that what was needed was a "third way." Not crusading reformer, not placating incrementalist. And not somewhere on a line directly between them either, because that would be milquetoast. The third way needed to create a new point of view and a new approach? *Optimistic intensity.*

This approach involved being an advocate for digital innovation at scale *and* proven efficacy in digital—to be laser focused on setting rigorous standards and measuring achievement against them at the student, teacher, and system levels; to be pro-teacher, pro-student, but really, at the end of the day, to be pro-*results*.

The team synthesized the truth about the protagonist here:

> An optimistic voice for comprehensive and rigorous solutions in digital education. Not about placating the status quo or being a crusading reformer: a staunch advocate for a third way.

The protagonist was not just an advocate for its own products—it was an advocate for anyone who was trying innovative technology ideas to help heal the system at scale. That was a key attribute of the protagonist: a generosity of spirit that needed to come through. This generosity drove one of the first external actions the new brand took at launch. But before we get to that, let's take a look at the fully realized story quad (figure 4-2).

Results and Conclusions

To begin to *do* this story, there were a few key first actions—naming, brand identity, and brand architecture. Naming can be fun, but it's also a huge undertaking with a lot of potential legal ramifications, particularly when you need a global name, so partnering with experts is recommended. For this project, the team collaborated with a firm called Lexicon. You might recognize its work: Pentium, Swiffer, Powerbook, and Dasani, among many others. After a thorough briefing on the project, they considered thousands of possibilities before settling on one clear winner: Amplify. The wonderful thing about *Amplify* as a name is that it is fundamentally about enhancement. It also reflects the optimism and positive mission of the company. It wasn't out to replace public education or eliminate

FIGURE 4-2

Amplify metastory quad

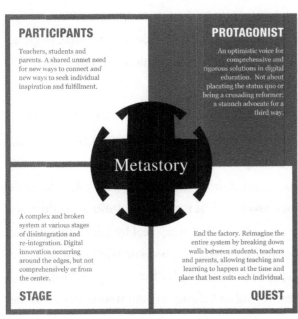

PARTICIPANTS

Teachers, students and parents. A shared unmet need for new ways to connect *and* new ways to seek individual inspiration and fulfillment.

PROTAGONIST

An optimistic voice for comprehensive and rigorous solutions in digital education. Not about placating the status quo or being a crusading reformer: a staunch advocate for a third way.

The insight that led to the Amplify metastory came from a comprehensive understanding of the Truth about the Protagonist.

A complex and broken system at various stages of disintegration and re-integration. Digital innovation occurring around the edges, but not comprehensively or from the center.

End the factory. Reimagine the entire system by breaking down walls between students, teachers and parents, allowing teaching and learning to happen at the time and place that best suits each individual.

STAGE

QUEST

 Metastory: Amplify is championing a root-and-branch reimagination of public education by liberating the power of individual students, teachers and parents with digital tools that allow them to connect, teach and learn in new ways. To do this we will:

the teacher. It was on a mission to identify and amplify what was good: *amplify* the power of teachers, *amplify* the innate skills of students, *amplify* the voices of others who sought to bring innovation to the space.

The name also helped bring structure and meaning to the various product components and business units that needed to be organized and rationalized. The team devised a three-part structure:

- *Amplify Access (the tablet business):* A platform to get new digital-education tools into teachers and students' hands in classrooms

- *Amplify Learning (the software and tools business):* Smart, immersive digital content and curriculum

- *Amplify Insight (the data business):* Helping teachers measure and visualize how their students are doing; helping administrators see how the whole school is doing

UNVEILING THE NEW DIVISION THROUGH PUBLIC ACTION

The first actions that any new brand or business takes are pivotal to how its story will be perceived. Since the protagonist, Amplify, would be an advocate for a third way, not selfishly advocating exclusively for its own products but for better solutions in education in general, it needed to make that story real by taking tangible action. The decision was made that the website would not be a pure product site but a place for advocacy for the entire evolving space— for others who were trying new things in digital education. So it became a place where anyone could go to learn more about the entire digital-education sector: who is doing interesting things; who has products that show promise; new approaches that are getting real traction and real results. (You can see this advocacy in action at amplify.com.)

The early results are very positive. The most important participant groups in the early stages of any start-up are internal. Having a name and having a story that they can tell with real pride and conviction has done wonders for morale for the whole Amplify team, including the folks from Wireless Generation. They are at the beginning of a long journey, but postlaunch, there has been a real change in the tenor of the conversations with business prospects, as well. The Amplify story creates the necessary insulation so that school administrators and potential partners can get back to judging the products and services from Amplify on their merits, instead of as a political hot potato. At the time of writing, Amplify has announced an important new collaboration with AT&T and expects to launch its first products about a year after starting up.

Five Things You Need to Do to Discover the Truth about *Your* Protagonist

Discovering the truth about the protagonist should not become a sunlit walk down memory lane. You should be as interested in weaknesses and flaws as you are in strengths and victories. For this to result in actionable intelligence, you need to build an honest and balanced assessment of your company. What is really going on within it? Culturally? Financially? Since Amplify is a start-up, there are no finances to speak of yet, but in an existing company with products already in the marketplace, understanding the financial health of the business is important. What are the financial weaknesses and strengths?

What is the general perception of the company, both internally and externally? Do you have a culture of fear? Hard work? Nurture? Do people inside the company understand what the company is trying to accomplish? Are they motivated? On the outside, have you been in the news with any notable successes or failures? Any indictments or pending litigation? Any notable product launches in the recent past? What is the authentic history of the company? Who founded it and why? What were their beliefs and principles at that time, and what impact did those beliefs and principles have on the company's behavior? Are those beliefs and principles still alive today? Or has the company evolved in some new or unexpected direction?

1 Do your homework. Read any and all existing material about your company: books, research documents, blogs, articles, annual reports. There are usually a lot of these sources around in a big company. Make a map of all your brands so you have a full sense of everything that you sell. A large retailer like Stylebox (see chapter 3) might have a thousand sub-brands living within it, so this can be complicated. Ask your research department for the data it has. Sometimes it's got great data, sometimes it doesn't. Look online for any information about the past or the present. What has been written or said about the company lately? If there have been books or white papers written, read them. If there are archival movies or videos, watch them. What is Wall Street's view? What is the media's view? What are employees saying online? What's being said in the blogosphere?

2 Interview broadly. You want to get a real cross-section of the company, from top to bottom and across the various departments—R&D or engineering, finance, sales, manufacturing, marketing, HR, customer service. These interviews should be one-on-one and held in an environment that encourages candor. Let people know that all responses will be held in the strictest confidence. You need to get at the truths here about the culture; the corporate goals and vision; the strengths and weaknesses of products, services, and people. The goal here isn't to get the company dirt, although if there is dirt, that can be helpful to understanding why things are the way they are and if there are changes that may need to be made in the future. The goal is to learn as much about the business as possible—culturally, operationally, and financially. Ask as many questions as you can in the time you have allotted, but the most important question is this: "What would success look like to you?" Ask people in the company to visualize the most amazing future that they can imagine and paint a verbal picture of what that would look like. It's generally helpful to give people a time frame for that success—over the next year? Three years? Five years? Sometimes it's a hard question for people to answer, which is revealing on its own. In a big company, there are usually lots of key stakeholders, and when we delve into a meta-story, we try to interview twenty to twenty-five of them if possible. Include input from as many disciplines as possible, since your metastory, once you know it, should guide behavior in every department and division of your business.

3 Leadership perspective is important. Sit down with each member of the entire senior management team. Don't do this in groups. Do these interviews one-on-one. People won't tell you the real truth in a group. This also gives you the chance to establish relationships that may help you make crucial, and sometimes difficult, decisions down the road. Start at the top, because generally, if the CEO opens up, that candor cascades down through the company. Once people know it is safe to tell the truth, everybody will talk. And don't limit yourself to leadership, either. Often there will be change agents or real visionaries inside a company who haven't made it to senior leadership roles yet. These tend to be smart young people who don't live at the top of the pyramid, but are people who get listened to by both management and the rank and file inside the company. During the sessions with the senior managers, try to identify some of these hidden people by asking, "Who are the smartest people you know in the company?" Or "If you could have anyone in the company on your team, who would it be?" Then go and interview those people, too.

4 Interview outside the company to get industry context and an outsider's perspectives on your business. Seek out experts and pundits in your field, people who are known for telling it like it is. You will learn a great deal about yourself from interviewing your own customers and even competitors or ex-employees if they'll talk to you.

5 Interpolate. The people you talk to won't give you the answer. Particularly in a large company, everybody has their own set of unique experiences. Remember the parable about the blind people encountering an elephant? Some will say it feels like a snake. Some will say it feels like a tree. Some will say it feels like a whip. It's up to you to step back and say, "I think what we have here is an elephant."

CHAPTER 5

The Stage

The truth I call the *stage* is so named because every story plays out on a broader stage, and the story of your brand or business is no exception. The stage is the larger context—the big picture (figure 5-1). It is the state of the overall economy as well as the economic conditions in your business sector. It is the technology that is currently available to you, your competitors, and your customers. It is the cultural context, as well: the music, fashion, literature, artistic, and political environment in which your brand or product lives. Are you in a phase of growth or recession? Who is in the White House or at 10 Downing Street? Are you doing business in an open or a repressive society? If you're a bank, is there a favorable regulatory environment? Are people feeling like banks are helping them to achieve their dreams? Or do people just hate banks? If you make jeans, what's happening in fashion, music, and culture that you need to be aware of and draw inspiration from? Being aware of cultural context is crucial to success. And

FIGURE 5-1

The metastory quad: stage

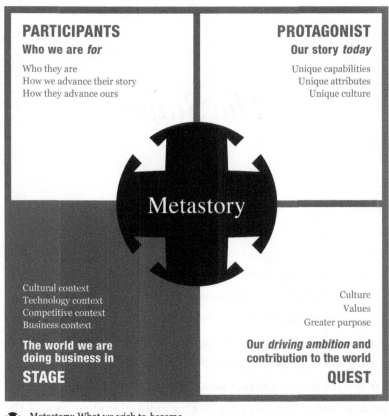

PARTICIPANTS
Who we are *for*

Who they are
How we advance their story
How they advance ours

PROTAGONIST
Our story *today*

Unique capabilities
Unique attributes
Unique culture

Metastory

Cultural context
Technology context
Competitive context
Business context

Culture
Values
Greater purpose

**The world we are
doing business in**

STAGE

**Our *driving ambition* and
contribution to the world**

QUEST

Metastory: What we wish to *become*
The narrative that will drive all the actions we take as a business.

probably the most important question you can ask yourself—right
now and moving forward—is how are you using technology and social media to better understand your context? Of the four truths,
the stage is the one that really enables you to tap into what's happening in society and use what you learn as leverage to get your
story heard and talked about. Placing your story within the larger

culture allows you to tell it in a way that will resonate most power-fully. Put another way, when you understand your stage, you gain incredible leverage to merge your story with the story of the world around you.

Spike TV Looks for Growth in the Mancession

Spike TV is a US cable channel that targets eighteen- to forty-nine-year-old men. And in the fall of 2010, it had a problem. While it had managed to build a $500 million business in male-targeted programming, other channels like Discovery and History had built much larger audiences with shows like *Deadliest Catch* and *Ice Road Truckers*, which were big hits among men and very easily could have run on Spike. Paradoxically, those shows were also attracting an audience of both men and women, which gave the ad sales teams at Discovery and History, respectively, much greater latitude in the advertisers they could approach and interest. Suddenly, Spike had two new competitors for the coveted male audience it had once controlled. Advertisers had noticed, and so had the Spike ad sales team. They began to argue that it was time to rethink Spike's story to grow the audience in two dimensions—older, better-educated, more affluent men, and also women.

The marketing and content teams at Spike were quite rightly concerned about this request. They knew that there could be real danger in abandoning a core position to try to grow a business. Niels Schuurmans, who runs marketing at Spike and is also the channel's creative director, knew the DNA of the Spike brand inside out. He and his very smart and dedicated team had carefully crafted the position of the channel under the line "Get More Action." Spike's story was the story of the rogue male, a testosterone-driven philosophy that led to programming that unapologetically celebrated the alpha male point of view on the world. "Let guys be guys" was a phrase often used around this story. The development team in Los Angeles had gleefully embraced this story, and Spike produced a slate of shows that were full of scantily clad women, violence, and explosions (ideally, all in the same show). Shows like *Deadliest Warrior, 1,000 Ways to Die,* and *Blue Mountain State* became Spike staples.

Spike's largest franchise and a real tentpole for the whole business was its Ultimate Fighting Championship (UFC) programming, including *The Ultimate Fighter,* live UFC fights, and various preview shows. The UFC had begun life as an extremely fringe pay-per-view franchise around the year 2000, but through clever marketing and the help of eventual distribution and promotion on Spike, had become a huge business, both for the owners of the UFC and for Spike. By 2010, UFC came to represent a large part of Spike's revenue. However, as the UFC's deal with Spike came to a close, the network realized paying the higher license fees the UFC was now asking would no longer make economic sense.

Spike also faced some compelling challenges to its business model as audiences spent more time on Facebook and the internet in general. As viewing habits changed from single-screen to multiscreen viewing, Spike had yet to define a multiscreen content strategy and business model, so it risked being left behind.

The challenges were huge. And while Schuurmans and his team saw the potential upside for Spike in broadening the audience, they also saw the trap: by trying to be all things to all people, Spike could easily wind up representing nothing to anyone. So the question was, how could Spike grow its business without diluting its story?

Spike was right to be wary of dilution. But a deeper look at the numbers revealed that while its stated target was men aged eighteen to forty-nine, it was really attracting men aged twelve to twenty-four in C and D counties (low-population-density counties outside of major metropolitan areas). Spike's current core audience was substantially younger and less educated than its stated target—a tougher sell for advertisers who want to reach people with as much disposable income as possible. This discovery had an upside, though, because it meant that there were huge areas for growth for Spike, even among men. And if it could crack the code on how to get women to watch alongside the guys, the potential for business upside was staggering. Further, there were some really compelling trends in the world—the stage—that Spike could actually take advantage of.

Researching the Stage

The first step was researching the psychology of men simply by watching Spike's own programming. It turned out that Spike portrayed a particularly nihilistic and disconnected view of what it meant to be male in 2010. In Spike's world, men objectified women, drank to excess, wrecked machinery and relationships as often as possible, had no sense of responsibility or consequences, and reveled in the darker aspects of life and the universe. In this world, a guy's mission was to have as much sex as possible with as many women as possible, fight as much as possible, drive as fast as possible, discharge as many weapons as possible, and not worry about tomorrow.

The next step was to turn outside for deeper insight into men and modern manhood. Fortunately Spike's internal research group had recently completed their own proprietary study on the state of men in the world in 2010. What the team discovered by going through this research was that the actual mind-set of men was richer, more nuanced, and much more interesting than most of the current Spike programming suggested. It turned out that men were struggling with some really big issues. By 2010, for instance, four out of ten men in Spike's target had grown up in single-parent homes, usually headed by a woman; in other words, a lot of them were growing up with no male role models in their homes. Interestingly, more of them than ever were choosing to abandon the stereotypical role of man as provider and staying home with the kids. Men were cooking and knitting and book-clubbing. They were also parenting and doing their best to provide without complaining too much about it—complaining just wasn't very "manly," even in 2010.

There were definitely a few things worth complaining about, too. In early 2010 the United States was just beginning to emerge from one of the longest and deepest recessions since the Great Depression. And it turned out that it wasn't a recession at all, but a *mancession*—75 percent of those whose jobs that disappeared between 2006 and 2010 were men.[1] And 70 percent of the wealth lost came out of men's pockets. Simultaneously, women were really tearing it up in education and the workforce. In 2009, for the first time ever, more working women than men had college degrees.[2] And more women were entering the workforce than ever before. So it was a double whammy—men getting squeezed from both sides by the recession and by women who were now taking full advantage of the cultural freedoms they had fought for and won back in the 1970s.

The team began to sense that the stage in 2010 was rich territory for a new story to be told about men, and there was a huge opportunity for Spike to author it, drive it, and in doing so, transform its own fortunes. But intuition isn't enough. To get real conviction around a hypothesis, the team really needed to pop the hood and climb right in. To understand the full stage for Spike, they set out to analyze four distinct components: the economy, technology, competition, and culture.

THE ECONOMY

The team began by doing basic desk research, reading books and searching news sources on the state of men. *The Atlantic, Harvard Business Review, Washington Post, Esquire, Men's Health, New York Times,* and *Newsweek* were all helpful. Books that the team read included *Home Game,* by Michael Lewis[3]; *How to Be a Man,* by Thomas Beller[4]; *Manhood for Amateurs,* by Michael Chambon[5]; and *Shop Class as Soulcraft: An Inquiry into the Value of Work,* by Matthew Crawford.[6] Although they got a good overview, qualitative data, and anecdotal stories, the team needed more rigorous research. From a wide array of specialist research companies and strategy publications, they gathered data on the current state of men, including EPM Communications' Report *101 Charts About Men*[7]; New Strategist Publications' Report *American Men, Who They Are and How They Live*[8]; *Generation X: Americans Born 1965 to 1976,* 6th edition[9]; *The Millennials: Americans Born 1977 to 1994,* 4th edition[10]; and Berkeley College's *General Social Survey.*[11] From Forrester and Nielsen, they got very helpful reports on the current state of men. But it was data from the US Census Bureau that gave them insight into their real economic situation and highlighted that the mancession was going on; specifically, *Income and Poverty in the United States: 2010*[12] and the *Fact Finder Survey for U.S. Labor Force.*[13]

The research showed that the mancession was having a devastating impact on male culture in the United States. There was plenty of anecdotal evidence that when men lose their jobs or get a pay cut, they feel a fundamental undermining of their gender identity—it hurts them *as men*. This recession was forcing men to reassess their place in the world, even men who were well employed. There was a general retreat toward fundamental values and enjoying simpler pleasures and making the best of what they had. That meant that the laddish, celebratory, self-indulgent, and consumerist version of masculinity epitomized by *Maxim* magazine and, to a large degree, Spike was crumbling under the onslaught of this new reality.

Then there was the issue of women. Their narrative was one of gain. They had started to earn, aggregated, more than men, and their salaries, though still relatively lower, were rising. Women made up 60 percent of college graduates. They had much more sexual and social freedom. They could rock an abdominal six-pack just like The Situation, if they wanted, and no one would think twice about a young woman driving a four-door dually pickup truck with an extended bed.

Both the real and perceived gap between men and women was closing. Women's narrative of progress was mirrored, negatively, in men's decline. One scary side effect of this was the rise of domestic violence—up sharply over the past four years, according to multiple sources.[14] This was clear evidence that a significant number of men were suffering, and in their frustration, many were snapping and taking it out on those closest to them—their families. But this harsh evidence confirmed that what the team was learning was real and not just a fleeting meme pulled out of a few magazine covers or newspaper headlines.

TECHNOLOGY

Without a doubt, technology, especially in the entertainment business, becomes more of a business force with each passing second. What a technology enables is important, but technology is also one of the things human beings often latch onto to help advance their own story. The smartphone you use, the apps you have on it, the laptop you select, and the shows and videos you watch on it speak volumes about yourself to your peer group. So keeping up with what technology does is important, but even more important is understanding what that technology *means* to participants. Who is using what, but, more importantly, why?

The team immersed themselves in all the research available about Spike and its competitors. They spoke to the channel's senior executives, producers, and writers. They also talked to Spike's loyal participants (along with some people who absolutely hated the channel). The competitive analysis looked at Spike's competitors through three different lenses: programming, platform capabilities, and brand characteristics. In programming, they looked across a broad variety of content gaining traction with Spike's audience and discovered that viewers were gravitating to "insider sports shows" (think ESPN's *Sportscenter* and the *Sunday Night NFL Pre-Kick* on NBC), "manly vocations shows" (such as History's *Ice Road Truckers* and Discovery's Emmy-winning *Deadliest Catch*), and "with-wife shows" (like *CSI* on CBS and *Law & Order*, *Biggest Loser*, and *The Office* on NBC).

Researching competitive platform capabilities was also pretty straightforward. It was evident that in order to succeed, Spike would need to be a multiplatform experience—but multiplatform with purpose. The best-practice examples the team found were

HBO and ESPN. Competitive-brand characteristics involved an audit of brands that appealed to Spike's participants across six distinct categories: sports, comedy, family, education/discovery, music, and tech/gadgets. The brands included ESPN, Comedy Central, HBO, TBS, FOX, History, Discovery, National Geographic, G4, and Fuse.

The interviewing of key stakeholders was conducted over the course of two weeks. The team interviewed a wide range of candidates who played very different roles throughout the company—people from the leadership team as well as marketing, editorial, research, content development, ad sales, and digital. For insight into the participants, rather than do additional interviews, the team dug into existing resources, watching hours of recent focus-group tapes that the Spike research team provided. The team also interviewed several media buyers as they are a key constituency of the ad sales team at Spike.

The team was surprised by what they learned, particularly about the participants: Spike's current core participants, while young, actually weren't very involved with technology. Since they tended to be lower income and less educated, they were less able to indulge themselves with the latest gadgets. They were pretty happy with Spike TV, but interestingly, weren't really interested in the website. Traffic at Spike.com, while healthy, was transitory—people coming once and then moving on. The site did little to deepen the relationship that people had with the channel. So when the team asked current viewers what they wanted from a technology standpoint, it seemed that the viewers were actually pretty content with the way things were. It would have been easy to conclude that everything was fine and move on. But the team realized that there was a huge danger lurking in accepting the status quo, because according to the research they collected on the industry so far, technology and its adoption was the future of all entertainment. Television is morphing into the internet, and soon you won't be able to tell them apart. Whether Spike's current viewers were interested or not, there was a new world order emerging all around. TV shows had begun to transcend the flat panel screwed to the living room wall and were being delivered via gaming consoles, laptops, tablets, and smartphones. Set-top boxes, TiVo and other DVRs, satellite dishes, and even more exotic devices like Slingbox, Roku, and Apple TV were all contributing to the dissolution of the old television world. It was clear that participants increasingly weren't going to live in front of a television, but in a time-shifted, on-demand multiscreen cloud of choices for the technologically engaged viewer. In this world, entertainment brands that win will be designed from the beginning to be accessed from multiple devices, platforms, and screens.

To get a fuller understanding of the role of technology in the lives of men, the team first looked at primary research on existing behaviors, hardware penetration, app usage, browsing behavior, and technologies that have a large user base. (If you are doing this digging yourself, the best places to start are technology blogs like *Gizmodo*, *Mashable*, and *TechCrunch* and companies like Forrester and comScore.)

Next, the team took a look at technologies that may not have hit critical mass but would have an impact on the industry and the participants' lives or Spike's business in the near future. Here, they wore the hat of Spike participants and experimented with new technologies coming into the market. They also interviewed current Spike participants about these technologies, exploring together what life with them might be like. People are relentlessly curious and social animals and often find ways of using technology that is a surprise to its creators. Take SMS (short message service), which was invented as a technician's system for network diagnostics. It was only when super-keen early adopters discovered it and started to use it for personal communication that it flipped over and eventually became a core communication medium. Now TV itself was becoming social. So the team looked into some notable social TV startups: Starling, IntoNow, Boxee, and Viggle. They also looked one ring outside of the television sphere at companies that are building businesses based on social engagement and community like Klout and Kickstarter.

The team also looked further out at some early-stage technologies. These are harder to unearth because many of them are being developed by start-ups and are still in stealth mode or at the level of prototype. So the team leveraged relationships with the tech community through conferences, hackathons, and start-up events like Y Combinator and TechStars. The team also took advantage of contacts with the venture-capital community to get a snapshot of where investment is being made. Some of the most interesting companies that turned up were working in the social TV space, including a very interesting immersive 360-degree video start-up, unnamed and still in stealth. These early-stage companies are far from proven and no imminent threat to Spike's business, but it gave the team conviction that they had a real grasp of the nearer-term technology landscape as it related to men. From this, the team constructed a picture of the media environment that the average man is living in today. Here's a snapshot:

GROWING UBIQUITY OF DEVICES AND MEDIA:

On average, 20 devices in each home

700 channels per TV

200,000 apps per phone

13 million songs per phone (streaming)

25 billion web pages per browser

89 percent of young men have gaming consoles[15]

MASSIVE LEVELS OF ENGAGEMENT:

Men spend 139 hours a month watching television,
5.12 hours a month on the internet, and 10.6 hours a month
on mobile phones[16]

71 percent of men use video-sharing sites[17]

24 percent comment on or rate video clips two or more times
per week

55 percent watch short video clips on a computer two or
more times per week

MOBILE AND ONLINE VIDEO:

63 percent of men share or forward content to friends

2,905 page views per person per month (web)

140 million YouTube visits per month (males, total, US)[18]

Given the importance of technology to the future of entertainment, even if Spike's current viewers didn't care much about technology, it was imperative that Spike bring a whole new group of technologically engaged participants to the party. But technology for technology's sake is never the answer. The only thing that ever has or ever will drive adoption of a new technology in the entertainment business is compelling content—powerful stories and storytelling. Doug Herzog, who heads up Spike, Comedy Central, and TV Land for Viacom, is renowned internally for his focus on this topic. His mantra is, "It's a hit-driven business. Nothing else matters." He's right. Having all the platforms in the world is useless if you don't have the content. But there is a flip side. Content can be developed with or without technology in mind. There was a huge opportunity—no, there was a mandate—to begin to build a content pipeline that embraced technology. Spike had to begin to develop shows that had modern transmedia audience participation baked in from the beginning.

COMPETITION

Defining the competitive stage is more than just figuring out the other companies against whom you are competing for business. Sometimes your competition is internal—employee attitudes or behaviors that might be working against you. Sometimes your toughest competition is some internal barrier or cultural taboo—an invisible wall that you must break through to succeed. In Spike's case, the competition was both internal and external.

Tension and competition exist inside most companies. It's normal. Different divisions compete for budgets and time, personnel and power. But that tension can also reach unhealthy levels and begin to hold a business back. This happens most often in companies that don't clearly understand and align behind a single story. Having a clear and powerful metastory that the whole company understands and accepts is the best way to minimize unhealthy competition and maximize the healthy kind.

With Spike, the internal competition was between the televised channel and Spike.com. The TV channel was committed to create or license programming that would draw as large a male audience as possible. That audience could be monetized by selling advertising time. The internal issue was that Spike.com saw itself doing exactly the same thing. Worse, Spike.com had a separate budget, separate P&L, and a separate reporting line, and so it set out to create its own original content that would draw an audience to its platform. Rather than working together to figure out how their different platforms could deepen and enrich the experience that participants had with Spike content, the two entities wound up competing with each other. The result was that both entities felt strapped for money, time, and scarce resources with little or no synergy between the content on either platform. There was a real opportunity to modify this structure and the resulting behavior.

The external competition for Spike's audience was much more obvious from the beginning. As was pointed out earlier, the company had been alone in the young, nihilistic, male content business for quite some time. But it was now surrounded by competitors who had grabbed adjacent niches, and over time, some of those competitors, such as ESPN, had become absolutely massive, and new ones were rising all the time.

Finally, there was the most vexing competition of all: distraction. These days, people are less engaged with television in general. The incidence of watching TV while doing something else (e.g., texting, chatting, web surfing) is way up. At the same time, viewing of TV ads is down dramatically everywhere that DVRs exist, and since ads are what pays for the content, content takes a hit. Last, there are just so many new content options: online gaming, fantasy sports, smartphone and tablet games, Hulu, Xbox, Facebook, Twitter, Google+, Apple TV, and plenty more. This will only get truer as time passes, with more intermediaries between the participant and Spike.

The cultural dive is a particularly fun part of the stage to research, because you get to read magazines, watch movies, surf websites, and hang out in interesting neighborhoods around the country, trying to figure out what's going on in the cultural landscape. Spike needed to discover how the mancession was manifesting itself. The initial research was simple—the team went to New York City and took the L train, making stops in the East Village and Williamsburg. A close look at the young men living there was very revealing. Everywhere the team looked, young men were starting to appear a little old-fashioned—sporting muttonchops, heavy wool shirts, well-worn boots, and old-timey eyeglasses.

As the team looked deeper, they began to turn up even more evidence of a return to the old ways in many parts of society. They discovered a burgeoning butchering movement, where young people were actually paying money to learn how to take apart a hog in the traditional way. Mark Zuckerberg, founder of Facebook, announced that he would eat only meat that he had killed with his own hands. His Facebook entries began to include the occasional macabre "killed a lamb this morning."

Men were seeking out hand-stitched clothing made by tailors rather than by The Gap. Fathers snapped up copies of *The Dangerous Book for Boys* for their sons. The interiors of men's stores featured iron and steel, raw wood, and stone; lobster pots and antique shotguns hung from the walls; and the watches, shirts, and boots on sale featured huge amounts of handwork, with almost Old World–like detailing. Cocktail lounges featured mixologists with elaborate mustaches pouring cocktails of locally sourced bourbon, home-made bitters, and hand-chipped ice cubes designed to complement the whisky without watering it down. Bands like the Be Good Tan-yas used old-fashioned banjos to cover Prince hits. And a young group of accomplished session musicians called the Pre-War Po-nies reached all the way back to the 1920s, using ukulele, acoustic bass, and vocals to reach their audience.

Digging further into the broader fashion world, using dozens of fashion magazines, clothing catalogues, and the edgier blogs from around the country, the team concluded the trend was pervasive. A fashion trend like this is interesting, but it can be a symptom of something deeper, so it is important to understand the underlying cause. What was suddenly causing guys to dress like members of The Band, circa 1969?

Alongside this was the rise of geek culture. For years, geeks and nerds had been the butt of the joke. In the 1970s and '80s they were the dorky outcasts who ran the chess and AV clubs, were given swirlies or wedgies, and were left bleating plaintively for help in-side a locker after gym class. That has all completely changed. America has witnessed the rise of the geek god. This started as far back as Bill Gates, Steve Jobs, and Larry Ellison, but it is being car-ried on today by people like Larry Page and Sergey Brin and Mark Zuckerberg—personalities who have inspired scores of young men to pursue careers in technology and as entrepreneurs. Geek chic is now a force to be reckoned with on the male cultural landscape.

The conclusion from all this was that men were searching for an identity that many of them had no idea how to find. Some were looking for something long-lasting from a lost world, from the time when men, supposedly, ruled; from the age of their grandfathers, when there were great mechanics, woodworkers, and hunters. Some were throwing off those stereotypes and leaning into the future.

The team began to look at how this cultural data intersected with the economic news. They hypothesized that the mancession, combined with the rise of the independent, self-determined woman, had caused this loss of identity. And men's way of dealing with that was to do something women used to do—they were trying on new identities, starting with how they looked. Men were entering a period of healthy personal exploration. They seemed to be feeling greater freedom to do this than they used to, precisely because the rules were less clear. And for the most part, this was all taking place quietly. Nobody was really talking about it.

The team saw a massive opportunity for Spike in all of this. They were perfectly positioned to help men along as they went on this journey of self-discovery. Rather than being a place to go to escape into the world of puerile male fantasy—boobs, beer, and bongs—Spike could become a real utility to help guys figure it all out. Spike could become a trusted source for information, inspiration, and advice on what it means to be a man today in what is a new world.

Results and Conclusions

To give you a sense of how the whole story came together, figure 5-2 shows how the Spike metastory quad appeared at the end of the engagement.

Spike has a name for this new metastory. It calls it *utilitainment*. Utilitainment is entertainment with purpose, stuff a participant can use somehow. It is content that helps viewers better understand what it means to be a modern man. It might help men learn a craft.

FIGURE 5-2

Spike TV metastory quad

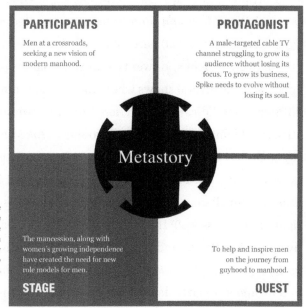

PARTICIPANTS

Men at a crossroads, seeking a new vision of modern manhood.

PROTAGONIST

A male-targeted cable TV channel struggling to grow its audience without losing its focus. To grow its business, Spike needs to evolve without losing its soul.

The insight that led to the new Spike metastory came from the Truth about the Stage: the culture of men was changing and they needed new tools to help navigate it.

The mancession, along with women's growing independence have created the need for new role models for men.

To help and inspire men on the journey from guyhood to manhood.

STAGE

QUEST

Metastory: The new Spike is a multi-platform service that inspires and equips guys to become better men by providing access to three things: content, tools and community. To do this we will:

It could introduce them to a new hobby. It might help make them better dads, better husbands, or better friends. It could be an app that helps them dress better or an online video series that teaches them how to interview for a job more effectively. Or it might just inspire by telling stories about other men making this journey, experiences from which other viewers could learn. Finally, at the level of community and connectivity, utilitainment opens up a conversation so that men can exchange stories and learn from each other.

Probably most important to Spike's commercial goals, utilitainment should result in content that is inspiring to both men and women, attracting a more balanced audience for advertisers. One way to measure success is to look at the audience composition of some of Spike's newest shows. Old Spike staples like *Deadliest Warrior* and *Blue Mountain State* routinely attracted audiences that were between 70 and 80 percent male and skewed young (median ages of twenty-eight and twenty-four years old, respectively). New Spike now has several shows where the audience numbers are very different: *Bar Rescue* and *Auction Hunters* have both attracted a 40 percent female audience. And two shows, *Ink Master* and *Tattoo Nightmares,* have tipped over to 50 percent and 52 percent female skew, respectively. That is a massive audience shift in a very short time. The median age of viewers of these shows is headed in the right direction as well: thirty-nine and forty-six years old, respectively, for *Bar Rescue* and *Auction Hunters*, thirty-three and thirty-four, respectively, for *Ink Master* and *Tattoo Nightmares.*

So while still early days, it appears that utilitainment is going to be effective for helping Spike to achieve its long-term business goals.

No matter what business you are in, it pays to go deep into the stage and really understand the broader cultural forces that are acting on your story. Often you will discover what Spike has discovered: that what is happening in the stage actually represents a great opportunity to grow your business.

Five Things You Need to Do to Discover the Truth about *Your* Stage

Understanding your stage requires observation and analysis of the larger cultural backdrop against which your metastory and the metastories of your participants are playing out. When things change on the stage, both opportunities and threats arise. Hummer's problems, for instance, arose not from anything Hummer did, but from a change in the stage. Understanding your stage will involve a lot of desk research. Much of what you need to know exists in freely available economic data and trend reports and forecasts as well as in pop culture media: books, magazines, movies, TV and online video, the blogosphere. But you *also* need to get out in the world and soak up some culture firsthand. So that's your first step.

1. Get out in to the world yourself. Pay attention to what you're experiencing in your own life. Go to where your participants are and experience life with them. Have you been to a grocery store lately? What does a quart of milk cost? Are restaurants in your area full or empty? Have you been to a live concert? Whose performances are selling out and whose aren't? And by the way, are you personally using Twitter, Pinterest, Facebook, Instagram, and Spotify? If not, you had better start. If you're in media, technology, or the arts, go to Burning Man, go to SXSW, go to CES, go to PopTech. If you're in textiles, hang out with some yarn bombers. If you're in automotive, befriend your local tuner club or hotrodders or extreme ecodrivers. You'll be surprised how much you learn.

2. Desk research: The economy. This is obviously something that affects every business and all people equally, your competition included. But understanding how it affects your business specifically is crucial. Read industry reports from Forrester and the government. Are we in a boom, a bust, or somewhere in between? How about your sector of the

economy? If you're selling heavy equipment, what's going on in infrastructure construction these days? Use public data, make assumptions and hypotheses, and test them against the data to figure out where the potential profit pools are located. This is mostly science, based on widely available data, but intuition and extrapolation can play a role here, too—for instance, in assessing new market potential, there may not be a published study about the market for orange-flavored pet treats. In fact, there might not be such a thing as orange-flavored pet treats, yet. But if you can get the data on the size of the pet-treat market overall and discover that there are, in fact, lime-flavored pet treats, you can make an educated guess at the market potential for orange. Think like a detective and extrapolate.

3. Desk research: Technology. Understanding the larger technology trends is important. But delving into technology usage by your participants and knowing what's coming next for your industry is crucial. comScore and Forrester publish helpful trend reports, and Gizmodo, Mashable, and TechCrunch are invaluable. Do an analysis of the technologies that are disrupting your market. That disruption will often include some aspect of social media, since that is the latest manifestation of the internet's ongoing disruption of all businesses everywhere. Does your company have a social media strategy? What is it? Who is in charge of it? And how is that going? What are your future plans in this area? How are you using technology to help your consumer actively participate in the development of your products or participate in doing your story? Is it working so far? If so, why do

you think it's working? If not, what's missing? Answering these questions can be as simple and straightforward as thinking about how you are using Facebook. Or in a more complex situation—if you're a running shoe company, for example—pondering a response to a disruptive threat like Nike and Apple collaborating on a technology/community like Nike Plus.

4. Desk research: Culture. PSFK and Cool Hunting are good places to start. Find the right people to follow on Twitter. And of course, relevant culture magazines and TV shows are helpful. You really need to immerse yourself in the parts of popular culture that are relevant to your brand or business, and increasingly in the networked world that can comprise most of that pop culture. But what's most important is digging into the subcultures—the smaller passion groups within broader pop culture that cluster around your products or your business. This is detective work, but it's really fun to dip in to some of these subcultures. You might go out and buy every magazine you can find about skateboarding or Japanese youth culture. Or you can get to understand the culture of collaborative consumption. Whatever reflects the markets you are looking at. You should look at art, music, literature, graffiti, gang symbols—anything and everything is fair game. Spend a weekend watching the relevant TV channels that may have some connection. Send some folks out into the world to do some ethnographic field research. Have them live with videogame players in Shanghai and bring that knowledge back. Dive into the blogs, as well (there's no shortage of those).

⑤ The final component of the stage is the competitive arena. This is where you take an educated guess at and analyze the metastories of all your competitors. Examine their products and their brands, how they talk, the language they use. Look at their packaging designs and colors, imagery, anything that has been written or said about them. You need to know as much as you can about the stories of the brands you will be competing against to make sure that you are crafting a metastory and action map for yourself that guides you into an open space between them. You might even discover that one of the competitors is so good that there's just no room left in the game. Intel is a famous example of a company that started out in the memory-chip business and realized, to its horror, that Japanese competitors were literally unbeatable in that space and that its business was terminal. Management swallowed hard and made the difficult leap out of memory chips and into microprocessors, an entirely different business. This is a truly massive leap of faith and one that could only have been made based on a real understanding of what their memory-chip competitors were doing. Companies hate discovering news like this, but honesty here will really ensure that your business is based on something that can't be duplicated, that is unique, that you can own.

CHAPTER 6

The Quest

The final truth we need to explore is the truth about the *quest* (see figure 6-1). As I've said, there is no magic to the order in which you pursue the other three truths. In fact, they can be explored simultaneously if you like. But the quest needs to be done last for an important reason: you have to have a real understanding of the first three truths before you begin the task of understanding your quest. There really isn't any more interviewing or desk research or data crunching that you can do now. After you have gone through the process of arriving at your first three truths, you have to take everything you have learned and turn your attention inward. Your quest is something that has to come from inside your company. If you work with an outside partner to help you develop your quest, at the very least the leadership of the company has to participate in the process and internalize the result. Your quest is the greater purpose that your company serves, the higher goals that you pursue—goals that transcend making money.

FIGURE 6-1

The metastory quad: quest

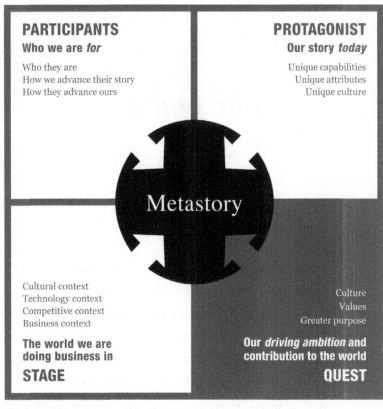

PARTICIPANTS
Who we are *for*

Who they are
How we advance their story
How they advance ours

PROTAGONIST
Our story *today*

Unique capabilities
Unique attributes
Unique culture

Metastory

Cultural context
Technology context
Competitive context
Business context

**The world we are
doing business in**

STAGE

Culture
Values
Greater purpose

**Our *driving ambition* and
contribution to the world**

QUEST

Metastory: What we wish to *become*
The narrative that will drive all the actions we take as a business.

It may seem strange to focus on something other than making money. But there is compelling evidence emerging that companies that focus on goals other than just making the most profit do better financially in a number of important ways today than companies that just look at the bottom line. In his book *Grow: How Ideals*

Power Growth and Profit at the World's Greatest Companies, former P&G global marketing officer Jim Stengel describes "ideals-driven" companies, and he puts their advantage this way: "Those who center their business on improving people's lives have a growth rate triple that of their competitors, and they outperform the market by a huge margin." He goes on to back that up with a statistical analysis of fifty companies that have a clear quest and over the last decade outperformed the S&P 500 by over 400 percent.[1]

Some companies start with a powerful quest from day one. Others never develop one. Interestingly, there are companies that develop successful businesses without having a quest, then develop one later and discover firsthand that having a clear and inspiring quest is an amazingly powerful tool. But the really important point here is that having a clear and compelling quest is a crucial component of becoming a storydoing company. Your quest is a central ingredient of the story that your participants will tell others when they begin to spread it across their network. It is the central wellspring of participant loyalty and evangelism for your company.

There are also companies that *have* a strong quest but have not put the time and energy into carefully understanding it, codifying it, and sharing it internally within the company. The quest lives inside an individual leader or a team of leaders who all resonate on a seemingly secret wavelength and finish each other's sentences. This is great, but it leaves the company vulnerable if that individual or team ever leaves. We see this happen often when a charismatic founder dies or departs from a company and professional managers take over. But even in a situation like this, the quest lies dormant and unarticulated, waiting to be rediscovered. An investment of time and energy in understanding, codifying, and educating people on your quest will pay huge dividends for your business. The key is to find an articulation of your quest that will inspire your participants—every company has a unique set of them—and serve as the motivating force to guide the actions you take as a company moving forward.

Shaklee Rediscovers the Power of Its Quest

Shaklee is a once-well-known company that had and then lost a visionary founder, lost its way, and today, a quarter of a century later, is successfully rediscovering its quest. During the early and middle parts of the twentieth century, Dr. Forrest C. Shaklee pioneered the growing science and business of vitamins and mineral supplements, became a very early adopter of an untested new business model, and blazed new trails in the then-unheard-of realm of social responsibility. But by the late 1990s, Shaklee Corporation's fortunes had stagnated—this once innovative and dynamic powerhouse and *Fortune* 500 company had become virtually unknown in mainstream culture and business. When it lost its founder, it lost its inspiration. As in many cases like this, the quest was actually still there; it had just gone into hibernation. The job of a new management team was to unearth that quest, reawaken it, and use it to revitalize the company.

The Shaklee story begins in the early 1900s when a young Dr. Shaklee, then a Midwestern chiropractor, became interested in new scientific evidence emerging about something called *vitalized minerals*. Though not yet part of the public conversation, it was becoming clear to scientists of the day that certain substances were crucial to healthy cell metabolism and that those substances came from food. Without them, the body became vulnerable to a number of diseases and maladies. As these substances were isolated and identified, they came to be referred to as vitalized minerals and eventually, *vitamins* for short. This discovery gave rise to the specialty of nutrition science. Young Dr. Shaklee had been an early and instinctive devotee of paying close attention to nature to find guidance in how to live a healthy life, so he was drawn to this new field and became one of its pioneers. Motivated to share what he was learning about nutrition and its positive health benefits, in 1915 he founded the Shaklee Clinic, a chiropractic and nutritional health practice where he continued to study nutritional science and develop vitamin and mineral supplements. "All I did was listen to nature and pass the word along," he once said.[2] That phrase became a mantra and a guiding light for Shaklee and the businesses he founded, and it still is, nearly one hundred years later.

After many years and several permutations with different partners in different US cities, Dr. Shaklee, who was both an astute scientist and an innovative businessman, encountered a second innovation that was to define the company's culture and catapult it to national success: the direct-sales model. He decided that his products would not be available in stores, but only through individuals who, having tried the products, decided that they'd like to become Shaklee "distributors," as they were called. Though not the inventor of this model, Dr. Shaklee was certainly among its first and most successful practitioners. Direct selling resonated with him immediately because it was such a deeply personal, connected way to sell things—you knew the people you were buying from and selling to. Dr. Shaklee had a personal obsession with the quality and integrity of both his products and the people who sold them, and

the direct-sales method meant that he would have a personal connection (even if it was through several other people) to everyone
promoting his products.

So, in 1956, the doctor and his two sons founded the Shaklee Corporation and started approaching people they knew and respected
to become both customers and distributors. Distributors could
earn money for both their sales and the sales of others they trained
to share Shaklee vitamins and, later, nontoxic cleaning products.
Dr. Shaklee's innovative company would allow literally thousands
of Americans in the post–World War II era to start and grow their
own Shaklee businesses, and by doing so, to have more control over
their financial destiny as well as their time. Being a Shaklee distributor suddenly allowed people who were accustomed to punch-
ing a clock to step off the treadmill. They could work from home,
spend time with other people in their communities, get to know
their neighbors, and spend more time with the people who mattered to them most—their families. Dr. Shaklee took great satisfac-
tion in knowing that he was promoting more than vitamins. He was
promoting a total lifestyle that resulted not just in healthier lives
for his customers but in healthier families and communities and a
healthier society as a whole.

The doctor was also prescient in his understanding of how human organizations could be inspired by the naturally "green" practices visible in the natural world. Today there is a rapidly growing
field of study that focuses on this approach, called *biomimicry*, but
he had only his instincts to go on. Taking cues from things like the
way ants recycled waste to grow food and the way lightning set forest fires that actually renewed the woods by culling damaged trees
and enriching the soil with nutrients, he developed a commitment
to green practices long before it became fashionable to worry about

such things. Nature spoke, and Dr. Shaklee listened. Shaklee later became the first company on earth to totally offset its carbon dioxide emissions and be certified Climate Neutral by the Climate Neutral Network.

Dr. Shaklee's beliefs in a healthier planet extended to his manufacturing processes, his packaging, and his products themselves. For instance, the company introduced one of the first biodegradable cleaners, Basic H, in 1960.[3] It introduced the first biodegradable laundry detergent without phosphates, nitrates, or borates in 1970. And it held a first-ever carbon-neutral conference, attended by some ten thousand participants, in San Francisco, in 2006. The company was also committed to efficacy and using only the highest-quality ingredients in all of its products, including its vitamins and supplements. So Shaklee supplements became the choice of many athletes who were trying to push the boundaries of human achievement. For example, Shaklee supplements supported the first American ascent of Mount Everest without supplemental oxygen, in 1983. The Shaklee company supported the first nonstop flight around the world, in 1986; the first human-powered flight across the Aegean Sea, in 1987. They powered the first crossing of Antarctica on foot in 1989–1990. And dozens of Olympians and elite athletes count on Shaklee products as a part of their regimen.

This obsession with doing the right thing for people and for the environment may not seem all that surprising today, given the growing recognition that we are witnessing a real, worldwide environmental crisis. It is important to remember that Dr. Shaklee's environmental efforts were taking place at a time when Americans still routinely threw trash out of their car windows while driving down the highway. This was pre–Earth Day, pre–ecology movement. Lady Bird Johnson didn't even begin her highway beautification program until 1965. Remember the "Keep America Beautiful" ("crying Indian") commercial?[4] That wasn't on the air until 1971.

Shaklee Corporation started off humbly, with just a handful of customers in the San Francisco Bay area. But the Shaklee quest soon began to resonate with people, and sales took off. The products were good, and the methods of the company were very human and inspiring. People would share the products with their friends and recruit their friends into the Shaklee ecosystem, and those people would sell to others, and so on. It was an ever-expanding network of sales, friendship, profit, and good works.

Dr. Shaklee was a visionary and a purist who believed that the true quest of the Shaklee Corporation transcended profit. He was convinced that the combination of selling products that made people healthier and using a system that brought families and communities closer could transform society and the world for the better and that if the company executed on that quest, the money would follow. He certainly had that right. By 1970 the company had reached $20 million in annual sales. By 1979 Shaklee had ballooned to $300 million annually and at its peak in 1982 was included on the *Fortune* list of the 500 largest, most successful companies in the country.[5] Although he wouldn't be familiar with the term, Dr. Shaklee had succeeded in creating one of the world's first storydoing companies. The Shaklee story was transmitted from person to person through individual acts of generosity. The company never advertised. It didn't need to. It was, to use the current Facebook term, social by design.

Dr. Shaklee continued working until he died in 1985, a wealthy and satisfied man. While the company survived this transition, it didn't survive fully intact. As with so many other companies both before and after it, the culture and goals of the company driven by management changed after its visionary founder died, in great part due to the fact that the quest wasn't understood well enough, or cared for carefully enough, by others. In March 1989, Shaklee was sold to a Japanese company, Yamanouchi Pharmaceutical Co., Ltd. The new Japanese owners understood the products and the product philosophy, so existing product quality remained high. But they didn't understand the quest—the underlying social mission of both the direct-sales model and the driving belief in creating balance and harmony with nature and natural systems. No real effort was put in to supporting it. What followed were fifteen years of benign neglect. Distributor recruitment dropped off; the distributor base that remained began to age. The company didn't die; it just gently stalled and then slipped into a long slumber.

The wake-up call came when Shaklee was purchased from Yamanouchi by dynamic American businessman Roger Barnett. Barnett immediately resonated with Dr. Shaklee's original vision for a socially and environmentally conscious company, and he believed that these ideas were even more relevant today than they were in Dr. Shaklee's day. He set about reawakening the company. It was a whole new day at Shaklee, and importantly, the company was living in a whole new world.

Discovering the Quest

As we have noted, to unearth and articulate a modern and motivating quest for a company, you have to have a pretty good sense of the other three truths already, so it is one of the last things you do. The quest is the truth that looks to the future and shines a light on the way forward. It is necessary to touch on each of the three other truths to understand how the new Shaklee quest was developed.

THE PROTAGONIST

As discussed in chapter 4, the first job in discovering who the protagonist is is to interview broadly within the company, starting with Roger Barnett, the chairman and CEO. Barnett gave generously of his time for this part of the process, as did the newly appointed CMO, Brad Harrington. The team also talked with heads of product development, distributor relations, legal, and HR, as well as key distributors and customers.

When doing this work yourself, you also want to dig into any existing data about the company. At Shaklee, the good news was that there were reams of internal research available. In many companies, you'll find that very comprehensive research is commissioned in good faith, but what you get back is a summary written by a junior research analyst. So it is important to dive straight into the primary data, if you can, so you can decide if you agree with the conclusions. That can be hard work, but it can be very worthwhile. One example of this that the team discovered at Shaklee was a recent report that contained about a thousand verbatim consumer responses to a survey about what people thought about Shaklee. The answers had never been categorized or quantified in any way, and they weren't in digital form—just a big (potentially very useful) pile of raw data. So the team took the entire stack of responses and categorized them by hand according to sentiment (positive, neutral, negative, or not aware). This gave them a really useful current snapshot of consumer sentiment toward the company. This was brute force work, but by diving deeply into the trove of data, what the team began to discover was really illuminating.

By going quiet for all those years in the 1980s and '90s, Shaklee was unknown to an entire generation. In hard numbers, only 20 percent of consumers aged eighteen to thirty-four were aware of it. This was going to make recruiting new distributors (the lifeblood of the company) even more difficult.

THE PARTICIPANTS

As discussed in chapter 3, the two primary methodologies for characterizing the company's participants were direct interviews and ethnographic research (the team lived with several distributors for a week or more). On the positive side, what they discovered was that the participants—people who sold Shaklee products—and the customers who used those products formed a community of true loyalists. So the active participants in Shaklee were still extraordinarily committed. Many of them had discovered Shaklee after having a life-changing health problem, such as diabetes or a heart attack, and they believed that the products had been so instrumental in helping them to maintain their health following their recovery that they had become lifelong advocates. Some of the stories the team encountered were heartwarming and inspiring.

The downside was that, as previously noted, Shaklee had stopped actively recruiting new distributors when the business was sold in 1989. In the intervening quarter-century, Shaklee had become an older person's brand. The average age of a Shaklee distributor was about sixty-five. This was a big issue, because these folks were literally the face of the company and with a sixty-five-year-old face, it was going to be tough for the company to speak to young people in a way that was meaningful or inspiring. Furthermore, technology use among the Shaklee faithful was low. Social media use was even lower than that. It was clear that Shaklee needed an articulation of the quest that would help to recruit a whole new generation of distributors into the company.

One obvious motivation for becoming a Shaklee distributor was making money—whether it was for a little extra spending money on the side or for achieving financial independence. But money was really only part of the story for the most motivated distributors. These folks tended to first come into the company as customers. They had a great product experience first, and then discovered and bought into Dr. Shaklee's original quest of doing well by doing good. They knew the Shaklee story and were active evangelists for it, often to the exclusion of other money-making opportunities. The key to revitalizing the business was to bring more of these folks into the fold as soon as possible.

THE STAGE

As the team began to think about where they might find these new distributors and how they might talk to them about the opportunity, they naturally began to think about the stage that the Shaklee story was playing on. It was an interesting place, to say the least. There were four simultaneous crises taking place in America in 2010. There was the economic calamity—record unemployment, including 18.6 million unemployed young people over age 15.[6] There was a clearly emerging environmental crisis, with deadly weather events largely attributed to global climate change—flooding and droughts, and the devastation of New Orleans by Hurricane Katrina still looming in memory—and other forms of environmental degradation (the *Deepwater Horizon* oil spill, for instance) constantly in the headlines. There was a growing awareness of the dangers lurking in our industrialized food supply, leading to both physical illness and environmental damage. Films like *Food, Inc.* were making a big cultural impact, and headlines in the media were full of health issues: obesity, childhood obesity, heart disease, cancer, and early-onset diabetes. And finally, there was an ongoing public debate about the impending crisis in the triumvirate of health care, Medicare, and Medicaid that threatened to unravel some of the basic social safety nets that previous generations had taken for granted.

All these problems were beginning to lead to a loss of belief in the American story overall. In 2002, 20 percent of people polled felt that the free-market system was flawed. By 2010 that number had jumped to 54 percent.[7] The cover of *Newsweek* on September 19, 2011, caught the mood perfectly: "Let's just fix it! Forget Washington. Everyday Americans can turn this country around."[8] People were clearly feeling that the system was broken and that it was time to take a step back and take stock of the things that really mattered. It was clear that relying on government and big business to take care of you was just not wise or even safe, frankly. People were open to thinking about their lives and their livelihoods in new terms. This was a real opportunity for Shaklee.

Another huge change in the world since Shaklee had entered its slumber was the change in the competitive landscape. There was heightened competition for *share*, both of mind and of wallet. As Shaklee stagnated in the 1980s and '90s, scores of new supplement companies came into existence, along with a lot of direct-selling companies.

But the biggest change was, of course, technology. On your smartphone alone, you could now download over seventeen thousand health-related apps, and most of them were aimed at consumers, not professionals. Young people—the very people Shaklee needed to reach—were more likely than older people to use these apps. And unlike previous generations, these younger consumers weren't looking for individual tablets or capsules; they were looking for total product systems that could guide them to better health. They wanted products, information, and technology working together. Additionally, everything in the world seemed to be turning into a game of some sort. Gameification was making technology more fun. For instance, there was a Pokémon pedometer for kids, called the Pokéwalker, that could link to Nintendo DS. Kids could train their Pokémon characters by taking them for an actual walk, benefiting their own health at the same time. This had big implications for Shaklee's product development. The company needed to modernize its whole approach to the category; instead of selling pills, it needed to create and sell entwined product and technology systems. Shaklee had embraced exactly none of this. Yet.

The final, perhaps most disruptive aspect of the new technology landscape was the rise of online social networks. There were flash sales, social shopping sites, and personal shoppers that consumers never met except perhaps via video conferencing. But the team was pleased to find that mothers, who had always been a key part of the Shaklee experience, had embraced the internet in a big way:

- Since 2006, the number of moms using social media had skyrocketed 500 percent.[9]

- An estimated 67.5 million women were engaged in social media.[10]

- The majority of Facebook users were women.[11]

- 91 percent of moms never left the house without their cell phones.[12]

- 55 percent had replaced the traditional family photo album with an online version.[13]

- 58 percent had fallen asleep with their cell phones at least once.[14]

Shaklee wasn't playing in this wondrous new field yet, but they were naturals for the game. The management knew a huge part of the answer to Shaklee's future lived in social media. The wonderful thing about Shaklee was that it already had that human network and the infrastructure. It was a business of people connected to people. And taking advantage of all those connections was so much easier than in the past. A Shaklee associate could leverage connections to a wider group in so many new ways, from Facebook to Twitter to Google+.

The other crucial aspect of social media is that these platforms allow people with shared interests to gather into microcommunities: people who are interested in losing weight, people who are interested in gluten-free food, people who are interested in farming, people who are interested in understanding the dangers of fast food. You name it, there's a community for it. The team began to realize that what they needed to do was create a system that allowed Shaklee to tap into this world in a meaningful way, and for people in these disparate communities to tap into Shaklee.

A NEW QUEST FOR A NEW SHAKLEE

With all of that input, the team realized that the Shaklee quest was going to have to work very hard. It would need to serve as an internal beacon for product development as well as an external beacon for recruiting the next generation of Shaklee distributors. This was not a time for timidity or half steps—it was a time for boldness. The good news was that it really was no exaggeration to say that every aspect of the Shaklee system could help improve some aspect of the problems that most Americans faced in 2011 (unemployment, lack of health care, obesity, environmental degradation, and disconnection to community . . . the list is long). As the team discussed these issues (quest development involves a lot of back-and-forth discussion), there were a few areas on which the conversation centered.

The first area was Dr. Shaklee's original intent for the company. Though he had never really written it down anywhere, there was a strong environmental and social mission to Shaklee from the beginning. This mission derived not from philosophical readings or contemplation, but from two formative events from Dr. Shaklee's youth. In his book, *The Shaklee Story*, author Robert Shook delves into both stories.

The first was that Dr. Shaklee was born with tuberculosis. The midwife present put his chances of survival near zero. But survive he did. His frail health as a youth motivated him to study healing, and he became particularly interested in natural healing methods. In his book Shook writes of Shaklee as a teenager, "Nature he observed the most and he came to respect it greatly. Not surprisingly he became fascinated by the healing power of nature. Nature has the ability to kill and to heal, he realized, but nature's ways of death were far more understandable than its power to heal. How did nature heal? Was living in harmony with nature the key? Was living in harmony with nature possible in the twentieth century?"[15] In many ways, Dr. Shaklee spent the rest of his life exploring these questions through the research facilities at the Shaklee Corporation.

The second event that marked Shaklee's life forever was that, in his twenties, he became interested in chiropractic healing methods at the Shaklee Clinic. As a part of that practice he had an X-ray machine in his office. The dangers of prolonged exposure to X-rays were not well understood at the time, and Dr. Shaklee developed strange lesions in his shoulder and in his hip. He went to the Mayo Clinic for a diagnosis and was told that the lesions were cancer and that both his arm and his leg would need to be removed immediately or he would die within months. Rejecting that treatment recommendation and turning again to nature, Dr. Shaklee instead put himself on a strict diet of fresh vegetables, vitamin and mineral supplements, pure water, and a vigorous exercise regimen. Within six months, his cancer went into remission and eventually disappeared completely. So Dr. Shaklee's belief in living in harmony with nature and using natural medicines and treatments for modern ailments wasn't a fleeting fashion. It was an evangelical belief based on formative life (and near-death) experiences. This heritage was a crucial aspect of the Shaklee quest. Even today, distributors think about what they are doing in much bigger terms than running a business. One of them averred, "There is nothing you could say to me that would shake my belief in the products. Sharing them with others is my driving passion. This really isn't work!"[16]

When Roger Barnett bought the company, he bought a business whose future he believed in, but he also knew he was buying a cause. It was a cause that needed to find a modern articulation, both to retain and remotivate existing employees and distributors, and to recruit new ones.

Another fact that emerged from the research, and that got a lot of discussion, was that a huge number of Americans today felt overwhelmed and a bit betrayed by the system. They had been sold a vision and a way of life that was starting to feel like a lie. And so they were tired, and they were guarded about accepting any new and unrealistic promises. The quest needed to be realistic. If Shaklee jumped out of the bushes and told people to buy Shaklee products and "save the world," the pitch would be met with skepticism, to say the least. So it needed to think about the quest in more realistic, more individually human terms.

The idea began to emerge around a new definition of the word *progress*. Americans had been sold a vision of progress that had improved their lives in many ways. But it was becoming increasingly clear that not all progress was *good* progress. Progress that filled the pockets of corporations and left the environment poisoned and lifeless for the rest of us wasn't real progress. Progress that allowed people to buy a filling fast-food lunch that cost less than a dollar but that over time degraded their health, their children's health, and the health of the planet wasn't real progress. Progress that employed people but demanded all of the time they might otherwise have spent with family and friends wasn't real progress. The team saw an opportunity for Shaklee to reframe the idea of progress in new terms for this new time.

A simple logic began to emerge: using Shaklee products would help make you healthier, have more energy, and create less environmental harm. Problems with your personal health would be reduced. The environmental crisis would be lessened, ever so slightly. Selling Shaklee products would promote your financial health either by simply adding to your income or, if you decided to work really hard at it, by allowing you to become a true social entrepreneur and build your own independent business.

If you alone did this, there would be a small but measurable impact on the world. But if more people did this, the effect would be greater. If everyone in your town lost ten pounds, health-care costs would drop. If everyone in your state lost ten pounds, it would drive insurance premiums down across the whole country.

The part about this idea that really began to excite the team was that because of the power of social networks, they could use data visualization to show people not only the individual effect that Shaklee was having in their lives but also the aggregated effect of the Shaklee ecosystem on their family, their community, the nation, and the world. This system could also be gameified so that there were clear incentives to pursue higher and higher levels. This logic led the team to the new quest for Shaklee, which the team expressed this way:

> Quest: To champion true human progress by amplifying the power of small, individual actions.

Encouraging people to join in and participate in spreading what the team began to call the *Shaklee way* became the new quest for Shaklee. This articulated a belief that anyone with any cause, no matter how big or small, could get involved in advancing the Shaklee way of living. The quest *wasn't* to save the world. The quest was to help individuals to take that first, small step toward a better life. If that were done well, and those individuals were then incentivized and inspired to convince others to take this same step, the world would indeed become a better place. If your goal was to lose ten pounds, achieving that goal had a positive effect. If your goal was to convince others in your family to eat less fast food, that goal had a real effect as well. By becoming a connector of people with personal causes to one another and helping them to dimensionalize and visualize the effect that their personal participation in that cause was having, Shaklee and its participants would make the world a better place.

One of the important actions that the new quest needed to inspire at Shaklee was product development. The quest encourages Shaklee to embrace technology in a whole new way in the future.

Using technology, Shaklee would not only begin to help people take the first steps to health but also help them to stay on that path. Imagine a pill container that begins humming a beautiful song or glows pale green if you haven't picked it up yet to take your daily supplement. It could even send you a text at work to remind you to take your vitamins with your lunch. This quest also leads Shaklee down the road to being a content company, similar to the path that Red Bull is on. In the short run, Shaklee can become a creator of what the team calls *snackable, shareable* content by making short, simple, and fun educational videos on a variety of topics (childhood obesity, the power of biodegradable cleaning products, losing weight after your second child by joining a walking club).

What the team loved about the new quest for Shaklee is that it returns the company to its roots as a pioneer. It leads to a future where it can break free of the world of traditional direct selling and puts it instead at the center of a modern, socially networked ecosystem of individual causes and positive effects—a story that is truly worth doing.

Results and Conclusions

You can see Dr. Shaklee's original vision of living in balance with nature embodied in the bricks-and-mortar of the Shaklee headquarters building in Pleasanton, California, today: it is an innovative, modern building constructed with sustainable building materials. Motion sensors turn equipment and lights on and off to save energy. Electronic window shades conserve heat but still let in 80 percent of the natural light. The offices were designed with an open plan intended to let air, light, people, and ideas flow throughout the complex. From every corner of the building you can see hills, trees, and sky. And outside, you'll find a landscape planted with the types of herbs that are used in Shaklee products. The place has been completely designed to reflect Shaklee's commitment to living in harmony with nature. Even in its time of slumber, the company had continued to do its story in important and compelling ways. But the purpose of a good quest is to shine a light on the road ahead, to give a company something inspiring to steer by and to work toward in the future. Now Shaklee had a quest and a metastory to galvanize future actions, to inspire others to do their story with them and spread the Shaklee way of life. Figure 6-2 shows how the Shaklee metastory quad looks today.

FIGURE 6-2

Shaklee metastory quad

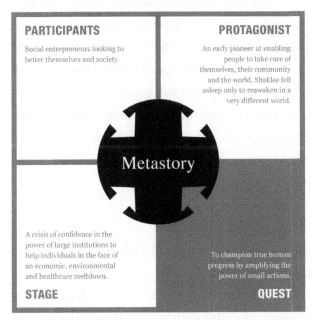

PARTICIPANTS

Social entrepreneurs looking to better themselves and society.

PROTAGONIST

An early pioneer at enabling people to take care of themselves, their community and the world, Shaklee fell asleep only to reawaken in a very different world.

Metastory

STAGE

A crisis of confidence in the power of large institutions to help individuals in the face of an economic, environmental and healthcare meltdown.

QUEST

To champion true human progress by amplifying the power of small actions.

The insight that led to the new Shaklee metastory came from the Truth about the Quest.

Metastory: We provide people with tools and inspiration to participate in spreading the Shaklee way of living. By encouraging them to take even the smallest action, we will help them to change their lives, change their communities and change the world. To do this we will:

Shaklee began to do its new metastory almost immediately. The first new product developed using the new Shaklee quest and metastory launched in January 2013. It is a new and truly modern weight-loss system called Shaklee 180—an integrated program of packaged-food products, a 180-day program, a mobile app, and a web portal that includes a way for users to share their progress across their social graph and encourage others to join them. The company wisely chose weight loss because it makes the Shaklee way something immediately tangible to people. Participants will be able to actually see it, photograph it, and pass it along.

There is one final artifact that it is sometimes helpful to create when you are developing a new quest: a long-form manifesto. After all the discussion and healthy debate are complete, and once your quest and the metastory that then emerges from it are crafted, it can be really helpful to write a manifesto that lays out the emotional case behind them. This exercise allows you to lay out the logic sequentially, but also to explore the crucial emotional and tonal aspects—the parts of your story that will touch people's hearts as well as their heads. It isn't for external publication. It is an internal document, a tool used to explore the emotional terrain of the quest and the metastory. This is an early version of the manifesto that the team developed for Shaklee:

Progress.

It's a word that gets tossed around a lot. But what does it really mean?

We can watch movies on our phones, our cars have brains, and we can genetically alter all living things on earth, including ourselves. Is that progress?

We have industrialized food production to such an extent that it now comes from places we never see. In our mind's eye we picture it as a happy little farm, but somewhere inside we know that the reality is very different. Progress?

Our paychecks increasingly come from companies headquartered in distant cities, run by people we will never meet. If we're lucky they even cover our health care. Until we get sick. Progress?

The average American spends more time working today than they did in 1950.[17] Yet the length of the average family vacation has dropped by 40 percent.[18] Progress?

Don't get us wrong, here. There are many things about our lives that are vastly better in the modern world. But it has to be said that as a society all this "progress" has led us down a few blind alleys. Sorry, but there's nothing happy about a Happy Meal and if you have to call it "Cheese Food," we're fairly certain it isn't either.

It's easy to get so distracted by all the "progress" that one day we wake up and think, wait . . . what happened to the stuff that really matters?

Things like time with our family and friends. Things like being in control of our own financial destiny. Things like not just living longer, but living better.

At Shaklee we're actually big fans of progress. True human progress. The kind that brings families and communities together, allows them to take control of their own financial destiny, their health, and the health of our planet. The kind of progress that leads to a brighter tomorrow for all living things.

Which is why at Shaklee, we don't think of ourselves as making products. Oh, sure, we make supplements and cleansers, some of the best in the world, but what Shaklee really makes is community. A community that shares a vision that began with Dr. Shaklee over 50 years ago. A vision that is more alive, more relevant today than ever before.

It's pretty simple. Little things matter. Small actions today lead to big results tomorrow. One less French fry and one more multivitamin. A day spent with your family, instead of at the office. One biodegradable cleaner instead of your usual. And, wow, does it add up over time. Better health. Time with the people you care about the most. Self-sufficiency for some. A cleaner planet and a brighter future for all.

Anyone is welcome to join in, in even the smallest of ways. Watch a video at Shaklee.com and you're part of it. Use a product and you're affecting the world in a positive way. Share a product and the effect multiplies. And little by little, we change the world.

That's real progress. That's what we call the Shaklee way.

Five Things You Need to Do to Discover the Truth about *Your* Quest

The work of arriving at your quest is mostly internal and should be done last. It is the final truth before you move to articulating your metastory. It requires both introspection and real commitment from senior management, and it involves asking some pretty fundamental questions: What are you passionate about? How do you want your contributions to be remembered? Time spent here getting real internal alignment around a motivating quest pays huge dividends down the line, because businesses with a powerful and motivating quest are invaluable to participants for doing their personal true story.

You *can* partner with outside consultants to work on your quest with you, as long as the top management of the company is prepared to participate and to embrace and evangelize the results. Of all the truths, a powerful quest can become the engine of your company. It can transform customers and employees into fans and evangelists. Here are some things that are helpful to think about and consider as you develop your own quest:

1. Become the person in your company who knows more about its history than anyone else. If it's an old company, read everything you can find. If the founder of your company is still living, try to get a meeting. Ask him or her about the original motivation to start the business. What was the original vision? Does the company have a compelling mission in the world today that transcends profitability? How is the business influencing people's lives in a positive way? How does the company want to contribute to the greater good? A great way to begin this work is to write down as many of the actions the company has taken in the last few years that you can remember. Hiring, firing, advertising run, products launched or discontinued, philanthropy, press releases, scandals, acquisitions . . . everything. Write it all down. Now look at it and make it into a story. This may seem hard at first. But let yourself go a little. What's the story that emerges from all of these actions? A really honest assessment helps. And if the answer is, there's no real coherent

story here, or the story is "We grew" or "We created share-holder value," then fine. You may be discovering that you don't have a quest yet. That's just an area that will need to be worked on.

2. Spend some time really thinking about your own motiva-tions as a leader or as a leadership team. What human need are you trying to meet? Is there a wrong you are trying to right? An injustice or a condition that you'd like to address through your work? What inspires you? A motivating and inspiring quest can be a powerful galvanizing force for any business, both internally and externally. But there is an even more important reason to define a truly motivating quest— businesses that don't have them are considerably less useful to people for advancing their personal metastory. You will find, conversely, that companies that are story-led from the beginning tend to have a powerful quest from day one. Google didn't set out to make as much money as possible. It set out to "index and organize all the world's information and make it useful to people." JetBlue didn't set out to make as much money as possible or become the largest airline in the world. It set out to "bring the humanity back to air travel." Companies with quests that are clear and motivat-ing create almost unbelievable levels of loyalty and passion among participants.

3. If you discover you don't have a quest, or that your quest has become buried or gone into hibernation, take heart. A quest can develop in a company that never had one before, and it can be reawakened in a company where it sleeps. But this does require focus and a willingness to embrace change. A

great example of this comes from the story of Ray Anderson. From the day he founded it, and for the first twenty years of its existence, Ray Anderson's company, Interface, was an average carpet and textile manufacturer, with no real quest other than to make a profit. But in the early 1990s, Anderson began to learn about the negative impact his industry was having on the environment. So in 1994, he decided on a big change: Interface would pursue the quest to be the first company of its kind to have zero environmental impact. That's an audacious quest, one that Interface hasn't reached yet, even today. But by 2009, Anderson estimated that Interface was more than halfway toward the vision of "Mission Zero," the company's promise: to eliminate any negative impact it may have on the environment by the year 2020 through the redesign of processes and products, the pioneering of new technologies, and efforts to reduce or eliminate waste and harmful emissions while increasing the use of renewable materials and sources of energy. The point is, even if it never gets to zero, by pursuing this quest Interface has made massive strides and has become a beacon for the entire industry to steer by.

④ To develop or reawaken a quest, a great first step is often to define an enemy. Hopelessness, humorlessness, pollution, obesity, big oil, big sugar, Detroit, cynicism ... almost any enemy will do. To align a group of people in a particular direction, defining who or what they are fighting against is a powerful motivator. Start by looking in your own backyard. As Anderson did, often you can find an enemy within your own current business practices. If you're a banana company, are your bananas organic or fair trade? Are your employees on the line or in the fields treated well? If they aren't, what are the plans to fix that problem? Like it or not, this is part of your story, and not fixing it will become more and more toxic to your success over time. The last thing you want to do, by the way, if you discover something about your business practices that you don't like, is to try to cover the problem up by proclaiming a grand new quest but not really addressing the issue. As BP learned in the aftermath of the *Deepwater Horizon* debacle, there is special disgust reserved for companies that claim to have some higher purpose or calling that turn out to not be practicing what they preach. Petrobras in Brazil is an excellent example of an energy company actually living up to the ideals that BP claimed to stand for, by the way. Its quest: to support the sustainable development of Brazil and every country it operates in.

Your quest can be a goal that you haven't met yet, but it can't be something you claim you believe in but don't act on. The transparency of the world we live in makes that impossible. The quest of a large, global sneaker company might be to inspire and empower the athlete in all of us. But if its labor practices aren't fair, or if its factories pollute rivers, the inspirational power of that quest quickly dissipates.

5 Finally, think about legacy—yours and that of your company. If you or your company died tomorrow, how would you like to be remembered? Writing a eulogy is another way to go at this. "Her stock options were worth more than the gross national product of Sweden" or "We could see his house from space" are not what we're looking for here. If the only thing you can think of in a eulogy center on the number of people employed and the shareholder value created, it's a good bet you don't have a quest yet. Your quest will often be the defining characteristic of your life and the life of your company. It's worth spending some time thinking about it.

CHAPTER 7

Your Metastory
and Action Map

Once you have gone through the process of discovering your four truths, you need to synthesize it all and define your *metastory*—what you want to *become* as a business. It is helpful to actually do this in one physical space. Dedicate a room, preferably with walls you can tack things to, and put everything you have learned up on walls. This will not be pretty. It generally looks like a sticky note delivery truck leveled a magazine stand and then plunged through the side of a Magic Marker factory. It's messy, and there is stuff everywhere. But getting your materials up on the walls really helps. It allows you to surround yourself and your team with everything you have learned, so you can literally sit inside it and really soak it in. Spread stuff all over the tables. Get together and talk about it. Draw things. Take a break. Come back and reformulate it. It's a process of thinking, debating, and refining. One by one, you want to create a hypothesis for each one of the truths. Nothing fancy. It might be just a sentence. It might be a paragraph.

Rational and factual arguments are welcome, but soft stuff counts as well. Make this part about conversation and open debate, and mark up the boards with thoughts and ideas. In the end, what you are trying to do is achieve a thorough and systematic understanding of the situation. You want the big picture, the good and the bad. You want to map the whole problem and begin to agree where the real truths lie. You want to fundamentally understand the terrain, because you're dealing with something that is much more sacred and serious than an advertising campaign. You're dealing with the heartbeat of the company; you're creating the pillars that will guide all of the company's actions moving forward. Rather than saying, "This might be true," you want to be able to say, "This is so," and have conviction around it.

Getting beyond Numbers

Getting to your metastory is the part of the storydoing process that requires the greatest amount of subjectivity and gut feel. Some folks (we won't use those old left-/right-brain labels!) are just uncomfortable thinking this way. They feel lonely, at sea without hard data and numbers to hang on to. It's probably worth reminding yourself that you already know how to make pretty important decisions without any hard data at all. In fact, most of us make the most important decisions in our lives based entirely on gut feel. You didn't do any focus groups or commission a study to decide whom to marry, for instance. Trust yourself a little bit here. What you are looking for is a metastory that, as much as anything else, *feels* right. It should feel like a reasonable description of your company today and be a good set of instructions for future action. It won't be complete. It won't be perfect. But it should feel *directional,* and it should feel *inspiring.* In other words, it should feel like it describes a future that you haven't attained yet, but could.

You are *not* looking for a tagline. That's external communication. Your metastory is for internal use only. It exists to drive action. You are also not looking for a catchy slogan or an empty mission statement. You are looking for a set of instructions that synthesizes what you have learned of the four truths and suggests future actions that will differentiate you from competitors and provide your customers with a clear story to use to advance their own true story. You should try to express it in the clearest and most forthright language you can. Do it the way your customers are going to do it: observe the known facts and assemble something that feels right to you.

Chapters 3 through 6 each contain the fully completed metastory quad at the end—all four truths and the metastory. I would encourage you to go back and have a look at those to remind yourself what one looks like. To further stimulate your thinking and simulate the experience of creating your own metastory, let's take on a couple of hypothetical examples—Nike and Walmart—not through the eyes of the hard-nosed business executive you undoubtedly are, but through the eyes of the participant—the average Joes and Josephines all of us *really* are on the weekend with our families.

Nike and Walmart are two companies that have long histories and well-defined cultures from the storytelling world. And just like your company, they face the need to reinvent themselves for the world of storydoing. Step back and just take in all the actions these companies have taken in the past few years, the advertising you've seen, the press coverage you've read, the experiences you've had with these organizations in their physical retail environments or with their products. Then just let yourself turn that into a story—as you have already been doing for years.

When I do that, here's what I get from Nike:

> Nike inspires and enables athletes to explore and then crush personal barriers and limitations. We create physical and digital tools, equipment, and motivation for athletes to achieve their absolute best. To do this we will:

And to me, the Walmart metastory goes something like this:

> Walmart aggregates the collective buying power of consumers to drive real efficiency in the creation of all products, everywhere. The result will be lower prices, better products, and greater sustainability. To do this we will:

Did I get these right? Are they the same as yours? My guess is ours aren't exactly the same, but they are more alike than different. And they are certainly close enough for our purposes here. It would take long discussions with folks at these companies and a lot more time to really get these metastories ready for prime time. But as rough examples of what you are looking for in your own metastory, they're perfectly serviceable. Let me point out a few features:

- They are both written in an active voice. They are meant to be used as a tool—a set of instructions to guide future *action*.

- Nike's story doesn't talk about shoes. And Walmart's doesn't mention stores. Shoes and stores are actions that the companies have taken to make these metastories true and real in the world. But they are not confined to those actions as businesses.

- Both of these stories describe the motivations that led to what these companies are today, but more importantly, continue to drive what these companies will *become* tomorrow. Your metastory should contain instructions for what you want your company to become in the future.

Continuing the experiment, let's take these two metastories out for a quick test drive and see where they might take us tomorrow. Remember, your metastory becomes a filter that you use to do your story in the future. Based on the metastory above, would a line of Nike locker room deodorizers make sense? Not really. How about a Nike high-altitude training camp for elite athletes? Maybe. There aren't very many participants for an action like that, but they would be highly influential to other athletes, so as a way of creating evangelists for the Nike story, this project might actually make sense. What about a Nike training-and-nutrition system I can subscribe to and participate in from my own home? That makes a lot of sense to me, and I would venture a guess that Nike has already thought long and hard about this very thing. Nike can be a food company? Metastory says "Yes."

The point is, as a tool for vetting future innovative actions of all kinds, your metastory is designed to act as the first screen they have to pass through on the way to implementation. The next step in the process would be vetting the economics of high-altitude training camps and high-performance training-and-nutrition systems. But that's for later, when we get to the action map.

Looking at the Walmart example, should Walmart build mini-Walmart stores at airports? Well, unless that action aggregates consumer buying power in some new way, no. Should Walmart have invented Groupon? Yes. Why didn't it? Maybe it still thinks of itself as a network of physical stores. But it is much more than that. Walmart was the internet before the internet was invented. By providing massive scale and aggregating huge numbers of both sellers and buyers (originally into huge physical retail locations), it stripped inefficiency out of the system. When the internet came along, it was an opportunity for Walmart to transcend the physical stores and aggregate that power online. If it had thought of itself that way, it certainly could have created Groupon or a Groupon competitor—and maybe it should have created or bought Amazon, too. Maybe it still should. Again, specifics like that are all material for the action map discussed below.

For now, let's stay with the metastory. I'd like to draw your attention to the word *sustainability* in the Walmart metastory. That's a potential new quest for Walmart that wasn't present in the early years of the company. In the early going, driving customer prices to their absolute minimum was the only quest that Walmart pursued. But today, having achieved such massive scale and success, we see a growing recognition that the company's formidable aggregated buying power can be used for a greater good. Walmart has the power to push manufacturers of all kinds toward a more sustainable way of business. We see this new quest emerging in actions like creating the Sustainability Index. Sustainablebusiness.com reports that as of this writing, the Walmart Sustainability Index covers about 100 different categories such as apparel, electronics, and toys, and that number should double by the end of 2014.[1] Roughly 500 suppliers have gone through the evaluation process. Next year, Walmart will start using the Sustainability Index to influence the design of its US private label brands. That change will impact the company's supply chain partners and manufacturers around the world that contribute to the creation of those products, including China.[2]

If Walmart continues to pursue this path, it could become something much greater than a collection of retail stores and a website that offer low prices. Walmart could become a consumerist movement that people join and evangelize, because by adding their buying power to it, they get lower prices for themselves, but also make the future a better, safer place for their kids. The larger point here is that your metastory, once you know it, is the tool you need to engage in storydoing. Once you understand your metastory, the last thing you want to do is communicate it directly to people—it won't provide them with a story to tell. People tell stories about unique experiences. To harness the power of the "medium of people," you need to *do* your story in innovative ways. So the final and most important step in this process is creating your *action map*: a series of innovative actions designed to make your story real for people and to give them stories to tell about you.

Putting the "Doing" in Storydoing: Creating Your Action Map

The storydoing tool pictured in figure 7-1 is called the *action quad*. To use this tool, take your metastory and place it at the center. You'll notice that this time the arrows face outward, because now you are using the metastory to drive action across your whole business in four different categories of activity: your offer, your identity, your capabilities, and your culture. The action quad is a really handy tool to use to make sure that, as you develop your action map, you are thinking holistically about your business. In the old world of storytelling, you would simply have come up with a story you wanted to tell and then executed the set of deliverables in that upper-right quadrant (identity). But to truly engage in storydoing, you need to

FIGURE 7-1

The action quad

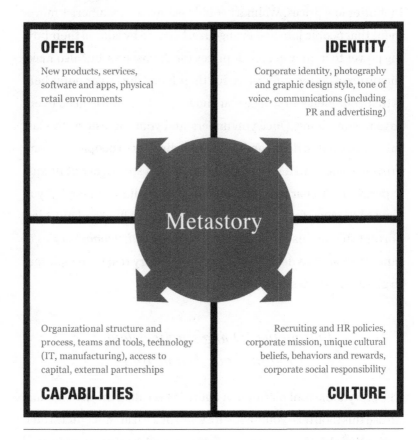

OFFER

New products, services, software and apps, physical retail environments

IDENTITY

Corporate identity, photography and graphic design style, tone of voice, communications (including PR and advertising)

Metastory

Organizational structure and process, teams and tools, technology (IT, manufacturing), access to capital, external partnerships

CAPABILITIES

Recruiting and HR policies, corporate mission, unique cultural beliefs, behaviors and rewards, corporate social responsibility

CULTURE

make sure you are using your metastory to inform and guide activity throughout the company.

Many entrepreneurs today instinctively understand the power of metastory and storydoing to guide the activities of their business. They live closer to the ground, closer to their customers, and they tend to smell and feel opportunities as much as anything else. Their decisions often begin as pure instinct, and the data is used to test the validity of that instinct. And innovation is in their blood—they know that to succeed, they *must* stand out. They have to *be* different because they can't afford hundreds of millions of dollars in communications to *say* they are different. The example in this chapter is devoted to a start-up business, and so many of the details of the action map we will explore are specific to a start-up. But it is important to note that the general principles apply to any business. At the end of the chapter you'll find a set of five general principles laid out clearly. By interpolating between the case and these more general principles, you will be able to create your own action map.

Reimagining the Future of Work: The Story of Grind

Grind began as an unnamed start-up in the co-working business, code-named Project Alpha. It really began as nothing more than a gut feeling among the founders: that there was a shift taking place in the cultural zeitgeist (the stage) around the idea of work. They had a feeling that the nature of work was changing, and that there was potentially a very big business to be built helping people work in a new way. These instincts led them to do a little digging.

What they discovered was that commercial rents were at an all-time low, especially in Manhattan. Gigantic office spaces were going for 30 to 40 percent less than they had been just a few years before, and a long-term lease would make these figures seem very sweet as the economy improved a few years down the road. At the same time, as big corporations went through repeated rounds of layoffs, there were suddenly many more people hunched over laptops in Starbucks, at the library, and even on park benches around the city. Wouldn't these people prefer a better place to work? Of course, there were already plenty of "temp" office spaces for rent.

But when the founders looked at these, they were unimpressed—*depressed* might be a better word—by the experience of these pseudo-corporate spaces, with their cheesy room dividers and air of quiet desperation.

The story being told in these spaces was one of defeat. By mimicking the typical office environment, they just seemed designed to remind the people who used them that they had left the sterile world of corporate America to enter something worse—a soulless purgatory, a middle step to their final fate, minus any job security. Amazingly, the founders also saw that these places were mostly full. Rather than conclude that the current model was successful, they concluded that this meant that there was massive, pent-up demand for a better way. They saw an opportunity to create a new and inspiring story about the future of work and to create the first global brand in the co-working space. They had begun to envision a chain of modern, inspiring co-working spaces across the city, the country, and the world.

Getting to Work: Metastory Discovery

The task then was to create the metastory and action map for this new brand. The metastory and action map would guide the creation of the full Grind experience, including elements in all four quadrants of the action quad: physical architecture; business proposition; corporate identity; naming; the look and feel of the first space as well as all subsequent spaces; the structure and content of the website; the content strategy for the Grind blog; social media strategy and monitoring; the PR and communication launch plan; and any necessary associated materials as well as help to implement outside partnership identification. It also included the creation of internal language and culture guidelines, as well as guidance on the content programming of the space itself—what speakers to host and events to house. And finally, since the goal was to prototype the experience and then expand it globally, the final deliverable was the business plan to shop to potential investors. Since the action map is an extension of the four truths and the metastory, we'll briefly cover the creation of them first.

GRIND'S FOUR TRUTHS AND METASTORY

The stage. What the team discovered was that owing to the dual forces of economic meltdown and a sense that the government was dangerously out of touch with the daily reality of the average American, people were thinking less about careers and the corporate treadmill and more about self-reliance. There was a growing disbelief among Americans in the ability of government or large corporations to take care of their fiscal future. They also observed that the new emphasis on digital technology was helping people follow this impulse toward self-reliance. Digital tools were finally delivering on an oft-made promise and giving people greater freedom and control of their own destiny. You could actually operate a pretty healthy business with equipment that would fit in an average backpack, and increasing numbers of people were doing just that.

This cultural analysis was invaluable, but the team also did a numerical analysis of freelancers' behavior, using government statistics and a report from IDC about the mobile workforce, which showed a potential Grind participant audience of about 28 million in America alone.[3] They also discovered a strong piece on cultural anthropology by Richard Florida, a well-known researcher and writer who had done a lot of thinking about the rising independent workforce and the new creative class.[4] In the end, the team calculated that there was a hard core of 17 million Americans who might be interested in the Grind proposition, especially if it were brought to their town. In the initial population heat mapping, New York, Los Angeles, Austin, San Francisco, and Chicago all popped. In New York alone there was a creative mobile core of over 300,000 people. And as of this writing, there were only 660 co-working seats in Manhattan and Brooklyn and an estimated total of under 1,000 in all five boroughs combined.[5] Clearly, there would be demand for the right kind of environment—hopefully, many of them.

The participants. Getting a handle on the participants was crucial to the success of the business, so that's where the team started. The total addressable market was large. But they realized they needed to tighten the focus so they knew exactly whom the story was meant to reach. They homed in on four possible participant subsets:

Ficus and a cardboard box (FCB): These people are recently out of work and actively looking for their next position. They want to get out of the house and to feel productive, but feel lame and out of place spending the day in Starbucks. Communal space offers him facilities, company, and a sense that he's not in this alone. While plentiful during a recession, FCBs are likely to pass through the space quite quickly.

Jet-setter: Jet-setters travel a lot on business and enjoy the perks of an expense account and a boutique hotel. They want to feel special and in the know. Today, they're working either from a hotel room or from the lobby of wherever they're staying while in town for a day or two. They'd love to have a space to use whenever they're in town, but it would be drop-in space. Must-haves: badge value and evidence of cool.

Dollar and a Dream: These promising start-up creators need a place to meet and to bring potential clients, but they aren't quite ready to take out a lease on a space of their own. They're looking for legitimacy, a degree of autonomy, and privacy. They'd be short-term members of the space, but as future employers and evangelists for Grind, potentially quite valuable.

Free Radical: These people are looking to make co-working a lifestyle. They have chosen to leave the corporate world to work in a different way and are looking for people who want to do the same thing. They feel as though they've discovered a better way of doing things and they're looking for empathy, someone who shares their attitude and outlook on work. They appreciate creativity, design, and attention to detail. They're in this for the long haul and would love a space with a little rock 'n' roll to it.

After much discussion and debate, the team homed in on the Free Radicals as the primary participants. First, because they would form a stable core to the business. Free Radicals are working this way because they believe in it, not because they have to. For them, Grind would be a lifestyle choice, not a temporary haven. Second, because if the team executed well against the Free Radical target, they would also get Jet-Setters and Dollar and a Dream types as a part of the bargain. There were other spaces in New York, one called General Assembly, that specifically targeted Dollar and a Dream, so the analysis was that there was less competition for Free Radicals.

The protagonist. Grind didn't exist yet, so obviously this truth needed to really grow out of the truths about the stage and the participants. Fundamentally, the brand needed to provide an attractive, supportive, and inspiring platform for Free Radicals. These people were confident, demanding, progressive individuals. A lame cube farm wasn't going to cut it. So the team began to sketch the characteristics that would form the truth about the protagonist:

Progressive: Grind isn't for beginners. And it's not for clock punchers. The personality is confident and modern, with some attitude. The space needs to convey immediately that it was built for people who are on a mission to change the world.

Friction-free: Everything at Grind should "just work." Details matter. We sweat the small stuff so that the people can walk in and concentrate on the big stuff. There's evidence of thought, intelligence, and care in everything we do.

Purposeful: Everything we do, we do for a reason. There's no fat, nothing there for flash, no chrome. Grind hates bloat and bureaucracy.

Constant improvement: Like Free Radicals, Grind is intelligent. It learns, adapts, and evolves as people use it. It's a space that will keep getting better, a space that gets to know you, a space that feels like you own it.

The quest. This one was one time the truth about the quest was pretty clear from the beginning, but the team's discoveries of the other three truths backed up and legitimized their early thoughts. They encapsulated it this way:

The end of working for The Man. To catalyze the revolution taking place in the nature of work and help as many people

as possible to escape corporate life to work in a new way—
outside the system.

The metastory. Figure 7-2 shows the Grind metastory quad as
it looked at the end of the discovery phase.

It was an important part of this process to articulate the
metastory in the form of a manifesto. This manifesto laid out the
argument in emotional terms and began to introduce specific elements of the *identity* quadrant of the action map—the language and
tone of the new brand.

Remember work?

The suits didn't listen to the T-shirts. There was a clock,
and you were on it. There were org charts and committees
and subcommittees of committees and e-mails from that
clueless guy in Finance. And at some point it became obvious
that the real lunatics, the ass kickers and the change agents,
the people who make s*** HAPPEN, were never going to win.

So you woke up one day and said to yourself, f*** work.
You stuffed your office in your backpack and headed down
the elevator and into the great unknown.

Congratulations. You're in. Welcome to Grind.

Grind isn't an office; it's the antidote to offices. A place
dedicated to taking all of the frustrations of the old work
experience and pulverizing them to a dust so fine it actually
oils the wheels of the machine.

A space that caters to Free Radicals like you. An idea that
puts the funk in funktional and some serious flow in your
workflow.

An experience built around a handful of simple rules: Be
ruthless about clutter. Abolish friction. If it ain't broken,

FIGURE 7-2

Grind metastory quad

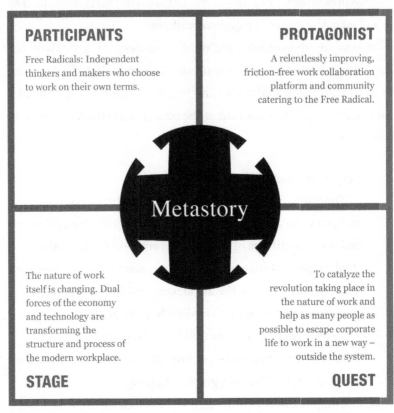

PARTICIPANTS

Free Radicals: Independent
thinkers and makers who choose
to work on their own terms.

PROTAGONIST

A relentlessly improving,
friction-free work collaboration
platform and community
catering to the Free Radical.

Metastory

The nature of work
itself is changing. Dual
forces of the economy
and technology are
transforming the
structure and process of
the modern workplace.

To catalyze the
revolution taking place in
the nature of work and
help as many people as
possible to escape corporate
life to work in a new way –
outside the system.

STAGE

QUEST

Metastory: Grind is building a 22nd-Century global platform (physical and digital) to support and inspire the Free Radical community as they collaborate to create the future of work. To do this we will:

make it better anyway. Sweat the details. Then sweat them again. And cling like crazy to the big truths: simplicity, community, work that works.

Want to shatter a convention? Rock an industry? Want to change the world? Let's get to work.

Grind. Work liquid.

The tone of the manifesto captured the voice of Grind, which by extension was the voice of the participants—Free Radicals. There was rebellion and some rock 'n' roll to it. It was essential to capture that renegade spirit to tap into the growing awareness among Free Radicals and potential Free Radicals that there was a movement happening here. The message had to be clear: radical change is in the air around the whole concept of what it means to "have a job"—making the leap out of a big company is something exciting and inspiring, not something to be feared. And that if you do it, there is a community of like-minded people there to catch you before you hit the ground.

Creating the Grind Action Map

As we have discussed previously, once you have your metastory, it goes at the center of the action quad (see figure 7-3 for Grind's completed action quad). It becomes the short-form set of "instructions." You can also think of it as the inspiration for the actions you will develop in all four quadrants. What happens next is a structured brainstorm to really begin to see where the metastory takes you. One important aspect to this process is that it is a team sport. When you build an action map, it helps to brainstorm with a broad cross-section of potential stakeholders in your company. The metastory informs action across all departments, so it really helps to have some folks from as many of them as possible be a part of this process. You have to decide where to draw the line, but include people who are experts in each of the four quadrants of the action quad (identity, offer, capability, and culture). It helps to have some outside experts in the room as well. You're looking for diversity here, a team that is more like Rocky Road than vanilla—a few nuts help.

FIGURE 7-3

Grind action quad

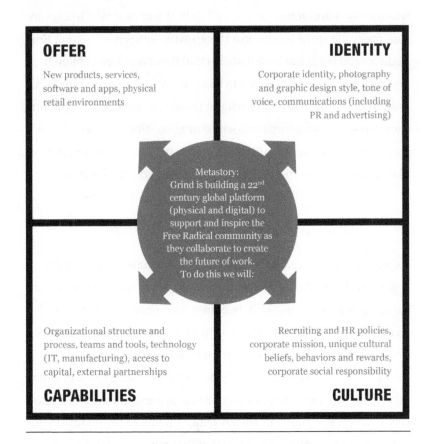

OFFER
New products, services, software and apps, physical retail environments

IDENTITY
Corporate identity, photography and graphic design style, tone of voice, communications (including PR and advertising)

Metastory:
Grind is building a 22nd century global platform (physical and digital) to support and inspire the Free Radical community as they collaborate to create the future of work. To do this we will:

Organizational structure and process, teams and tools, technology (IT, manufacturing), access to capital, external partnerships

CAPABILITIES

Recruiting and HR policies, corporate mission, unique cultural beliefs, behaviors and rewards, corporate social responsibility

CULTURE

For example, the Grind session was about the future of work. So, in addition to founders Stuart and Karina Warshaw, who had backgrounds in business and sustainable design, respectively, and Benjamin Dyett, whose background was in real estate law, the team invited Scott Belsky, founder of The Behance Network and The 99Uconference. Belsky is a published author and an expert in helping creative people become more productive in their work. Grind was a potential media space, so the team invited Josh Rubin. Rubin was cofounder of the culture and design blog Cool Hunting, as well as the promotion and partnership company Largetail, which specializes in creating unusual technology and media partnerships. Because Grind needed to be both a digital and a physical platform, the team invited Josh Campbell, founder of the web design firm Magic+Might, and architects Don Shillingburg and Vincent Bandy. Technology would be critical to creating a better experience at Grind, so the team invited Andrew Zolty and Michael Lipton from the creative technology company Breakfast. And the team knew that eventually they might need to raise some capital to scale the business, so they invited venture capitalist Mark Alison, founder of New York Angels, one of the most successful angel investment funds in the world. The team also included advertising copywriter Stuart Mickle and design guru Peter Sunna. The proceedings were moderated by strategist Steve Walls. It was a profoundly talented and creative group of people.

Discovering the Grind Action Principles

As illustrated in the Nike and Walmart examples at the beginning of the chapter, when you ask it to, your metastory will begin to suggest future ideas to you—concrete actions the company can take in each of the quadrants. But you are *also* looking for a set of something called *action principles*. These are not specific ideas but rather a more specific set of guidelines that can be used to help guide future ideation. It would be great if the process of coming up with actions and action principles were neat and clean and sequential. What tends to happen in real life is this: in the brainstorm, ideas begin to flow. And that's good. Let them flow. Just get stuff up on walls. You'll have ideas about color and tone of voice, and ideas for new products, and ideas for places to open future locations and new technologies you want to embrace. It should be a really diverse set of ideas. Once you've papered the place with awesome potential actions, you will notice that some of them just naturally want to hang out together in groups. Some of those groups will want to hang out near each other as well. You'll find that what begins to emerge is something like a map of the universe, with individual ideas clustered together the way stars cluster into galaxies. And then groups of these galaxies will hover near each to form the four quadrants. To get to action principles, what you want to pay attention to are the galaxies themselves—the idea "stars" that form that galaxy are being drawn together by an underlying principle of the business. The natural grouping tells you that there is an undiscovered action principle underneath.

Your next task is to debate and articulate the principle. Your action principles will become very useful to you over time. They are a second layer of more specific instructions that underlie the metastory. People from different areas of the business can use them to guide and inspire ideas for new actions in the future.

It will help to get specific again about the Grind process: below are the action principles that emerged from the initial brainstorm. I have included some of the "stars" as well so you can see what the "galaxies" looked like up on the wall. Some of these ideas made it to the final product, and some did not, but the action principles (in italic) have become the principles that the team returns to again and again.

GRIND ACTION PRINCIPLES:

We're from the future. Our design aesthetic is modern, un-cluttered: Vitra, not shabby chic. Our technology is the best available: the latest Macs, enough Wi-Fi bandwidth to run a home shopping network over it. Our "gallery wall" magi-cally becomes your portfolio display with a tap of your RFID Grind ID card.

We have an attitude. Like the Free Radicals we serve, we've busted down the wall of our stall and galloped into the forest. There is a rawness and wildness just beneath the surface. An impatience with the status quo. An eagerness about what's next. We swear occasionally, and we don't apologize for it.

We worship functionality. Simple is good. In our conference rooms, AV equipment has three buttons: "On, Off, and Help." The rooms are set up to get you Skyping, presenting, and hooked up with the minimum of BS. We have every dongle known to man, and a somebody who knows how to use them.

We sweat the details. There's evidence of thoughtfulness in all that we do. Power connections are at table height, not on the floor. A "zero-gravity clutter" system whisks your stuff (your backpack, your shopping, your bike helmet) to the ceiling—clearing up more space for you and others. A Muji vending machine saves you from having to bum a pen and a pad from the person next to you.

We have your back. We're here to make it easy for you to work, but we're also here to help your business work. So if you sign up as a long-term member, you get access to our on-staff bookkeeper, to our on-staff legal team, and to our "black book" of useful suppliers and forms.

We are transparent. You can see everything you need to see at one glance—where an empty seat is, where resources are, how things work (open plan). Nothing's hidden, including fees.

The work comes first. Open plan doesn't mean anything goes. Sound cones keep music in one area. Booths keep phone calls private. And every desk has a "not now, I'm busy" button that you can hit to make sure you're not disturbed.

Grind is yours. Customize the rooms that you use (Skype, conference, chill-out space) using video projections that can turn a wall into your logo, a forest, or a beach, depending on your mood and what you need the space to do for you. Want to change a policy? Take it up with the Grindist council.

Using the Action Quadrants to Organize Your Action Map

Once you have this work done, and you are happy with your action principles, it is time to set about vetting the individual "stars" themselves. You want to begin to really bear down on the individual ideas and figure out which ones are realistic (desirable, actionable, and affordable). This is not something that can be done in a day. It is something that members of the team will go away and do alone or in smaller groups, and then come back and represent in a future session. But as a group, before you disperse, you want to do a thorough job of prioritizing and setting out the next actions for the group. Here is the action map that emerged from that process for Grind, organized by quadrant.

Naming. We've been using the name *Grind* from the beginning in this chapter, but the name needed to flow from the metastory, so the project was unnamed until we got to this point in the process. Hundreds of names were generated in the brainstorm. They ran the gamut from business metaphors like Lemonade Stand and references to the cubicle farms like Ubical. It was kind of hard to tell where some of the others came from. Horses & Cows, for instance (one too many nuts on that one, for sure). It was a fun process churning out huge numbers of names and then sifting and winnowing, deliberating and debating. One that kept coming up was "Grind." There was a lot of debate around that one, for obvious reasons—it is the word for the most soul-crushing aspects of a bad work experience. But it also means to smooth down, to reduce. And that's what this business was going to do: make work easier. So, perversely, it really embraces the vision for the business. It was monosyllabic, had texture, and seemed a bit sarcastic—an ironic critique of the old way of working. Perfect.

Language and design. Language and design are crucial to the overall Grind experience. As you have gathered by now, Grind has an attitude. The team wanted that attitude to peek through into the space itself. But they didn't want to overdesign it to the point where people would get tired of it. This phase of the project required collaboration between writer Stuart Mickle, architect Vincent Bandy,

FIGURE 7-4

Grind logo

and designer Peter Sunna. Sunna created the Grind corporate identity, which was primarily white, gray, and orange.

He created the logo by setting the word *Grind* in a very common
typeface, Futura Extra Bold, and grinding the corners off it to create a customized piece of typography that had the story of the business baked into it (figure 7-4). The conference rooms themselves
had inspiring names: *Think Tank* and *Do Tank*.

Work Liquid. Stuart Mickle was the keeper of the Grind voice.
He wrote the manifesto as well as penning the Grind tagline: *Work
Liquid*. Work Liquid is much more than a slogan. It is a supercom-
pact form of the entire belief system of the company. It's also a measuring stick for future actions: if it doesn't help you or inspire you
in some way to Work Liquid, it just isn't Grindworthy.

Grindisms. Stuart also created a series of Grindisms: short,
pithy statements that might wind up on a T-shirt or a poster that
reminded people of important aspects of the Grind culture and
philosophy.

More balls. Less chains.

Come. Sit. Conquer.

Unwork in progress.

You used to have a job, but we won't hold it against you.

Abolish friction.

Love what you do or do something else.

Nobody's ever won a rat race.

If today feels just like yesterday, something is wrong.

F**k committees. I like lunatics.

That last is a quote from the late, great designer and provocateur Tibor Kalman. I like to think that Tibor would have liked Grind a lot.

OFFER

The physical space. For the overall aesthetic in the space, architect Vincent Bandy went for a modern, open plan, with beautifully polished concrete floors and communal seating. White walls and black or dark gray furniture set the baseline. Peter Sunna then began to introduce a few splashes of color in the space, beginning with a really clever mural of Work Liquid, painted in a way that made it a piece of abstract art unless you viewed it from a precise spot in the room, at which point it became perfectly legible. Sunna also came up with the idea of ghosting clichéd corporate phrases on the glass walls and doors of the conference rooms. The translucent typography applied directly to the glass in these rooms gave them a more private feeling when you were inside them, and the words took a sly shot at the world of "old work." Instead of a typical corporate Grind logo affixed to the wall in reception, Mickle and Sunna created a "moving logo" on a video monitor. The logo is front and center, but behind it is a thirty-minute loop of archival film footage of the old way of working. Like the name, Grind, this footage uses negative imagery to make a positive statement: "We are free!" The philosophy extended to the smallest details in the space. In both bathrooms, there were reminders that "Grindists are encouraged to wash their hands of the 'old work' experience." And finally, at the center of the room, the team commissioned modern artist and Grindist Justin Gignac to create a functional piece of art: a large coffee table made of a Plexiglas box that contained hundreds of artifacts from the old way of working: paper Rolodexes, fax machines, wired telephones, switchboard equipment. It was a sarcophagus for the past and a statement about what Grindists were leaving behind as they embraced a shiny, new future of work.

Frictionless check-in. The center of the Grind philosophy was *frictionlessness*. It was important to the team that the experience start with a participant's arrival in the space. The team wanted a customized experience that "automagically" made that person feel like an owner, not a visitor. Walk in. Tap your RFID Grind ID card on the RFID reader in the entryway. You get a personal greeting and—boom, you're logged in. Behind the scenes, the system keeps track of daily use and the amount of time people are in the space, allowing Grind to optimize the experience for you. For instance, participants can also log in to their account to check how busy Grind is before heading over in the morning. Check-in is also tied into the billing system, so daily members will automatically be charged through the billing platform. The system allows its users to concentrate on getting amazing work done while Grind does the heavy lifting behind the scenes.

The gallery wall. The work that Grindists do is incredibly creative and inspiring. Grind wanted the space to help members not only create that work but also display that work. The gallery wall is a fifty-foot wall that runs down one side of the space. On the wall are twelve video screens of varying sizes. Once they get their account set up at Grind, Grindists can use those screens to display their work. Walk up to the wall and touch your membership card to the RFID reader and the wall will display a preset selection of your best work. It can also display a particular set of work, so it can be used to make a presentation to a client on one particular project. When the wall is idling, it automagically scrolls through a selection of high-resolution images pulled from the portfolios of Grindists. Beneath each screen are two buttons. Press one button and a notice goes to the creator that you "appreciate" the work. The second button instantly prints a copy of whatever is displayed on that screen with full credits and contact information. So Grindists are incentivized to put their stuff up not only to show to clients but to market themselves to the Grind community. The gallery wall is designed to become an iconic fixture in every Grind location around the world and, as Grind scales, to become increasingly useful to members.

The Agora. The Agora is designed to leverage the power of the community in the digital realm and it, too, will become more useful over time as Grind scales. *Agora* is an ancient Greek term for marketplace. In ancient Greek towns and cities, the agora was a marketplace for goods, but also services and ideas. Speakers and poets held forth to the crowds gathered there. Major government announcements and political addresses were made there. And, obviously, goods and services were exchanged there as well. Need a great carpenter? Visit the agora. Need to buy a bushel of tomatoes or a new camel? Visit the agora.

In Grind terms, the Agora begins as a very simple member profile system. If you opt to make your profile public, your image, professional background, and contact information will be visible on the system to other Grindists. There is a screen in the space that shows who is checked in that day, and in the future you will be able to see who is checked in at Grinds all over the world. At first, this simply facilitates a sense of who is who in the Grind community. In the near future, the Agora will include a "I have–I need" functionality. So, for instance, if you "need" a website and you "have" a law degree, the system will help you match your "have" with someone else's appropriate "need," allowing one Grindist to exchange advice and services with one another, frictionlessly. Over time, the Agora can become a more sophisticated collaborative skills exchange. Ultimately, it has the potential to become its own internal economy.

#rethink. As part of designing the ongoing content and event strategy for Grind, the team created #rethink, a speaker series and YouTube channel. The second Tuesday of every month, Grind hosts a speaker who does thirty minutes on rethinking an important aspect of how we live and work today. Sara Horowitz, founder of the Freelancers Union; Fred Wilson of Union Square Ventures; and Roo Rogers, coauthor of *What's Mine Is Yours: The Rise of Collaborative Consumption*, have all been speakers.[6] These events enrich the Grindist experience but also get potential members into the space on a regular cadence to experience Grind firsthand and arm them with a story to tell when they leave.

CAPABILITIES

Intelligentsia Coffee. In collaboration with Cool Hunting and Largetail, the Grind team began looking for iconic partnerships—other brands that could be brought into the space to provide specific functionality or to enhance the experience. The first partnership the team put in place was with Intelligentsia Coffee, which would be a free perk (no pun intended) to all Grind members. After essentially being commoditized by Starbucks, artisanal coffee was making a huge comeback across the country. Intelligentsia was one of a handful of really meaningful boutique brands in that emerging space. In addition to making sure the coffee experience in Grind would be unsurpassed, the significance of partnering with the Intelligentsia brand would not be lost on Grind's participants.

CULTURE

The Grindist Council. A large part of the Grind metastory is that it is a community of like-minded individuals. To give that concept teeth, the team took the action of creating the Grindist Council, which gives six community members a platform and forum to voice concerns, brainstorm improvements, and guide policy. Over time, the plan is to give the council increasing amounts of input on the direction of the business. Grindists will one day really run Grind.

Results and Conclusions

The story of frictionless work for Free Radicals infuses everything Grind does. While not exactly iconic experiences, there are a number of other aspects to Grind that were driven by the Grind metastory. For instance, the team noticed that most co-working spaces had quite complex pricing, with one price for late-night hours and another for the day, one for sitting on couches and another for sitting at a private desk. They wanted to remove all of this friction. So, after a number of spirited exchanges between the team members, everybody agreed to two prices: monthly and daily. That was it. Likewise, they decided that Grind wouldn't reserve seats for anyone. They didn't want people to have to check in on their phone on the way in or call the night before. So the team settled on a very simple and, I think, quite elegant solution for how to seat people. It's a democratic technology that tells you when a seat is available: if no one is sitting in it, it's yours. Even the design of the lighting was thought through at two levels: first, that it is great for Grindists in the space, but second, it looks great from the street level, one floor below. The grid pattern is designed to become an iconic experience for passersby and will become part of every Grind location around the world.

So what are the key takeaways for your business? The action map is different for every company, but it is always driven by the metastory. And your action map never ends. Once you have locked down on your metastory, you must constantly be thinking about what comes next. For Grind, this will involve continuous innovation along three entwined pathways: community, technology, and scale. One of the big friction points for Grindists today, for instance, is physical availability. Having one Grind is good. But a Grind location is a little like a phone—the more of them that exist in the world, the more useful they all become. Grindists travel, and so availability in cities they travel to and from frequently will remove friction from their lives. Proliferation of locations is more than a financial imperative, it is a *metastory* imperative—the story becomes more true the more of them there are. The second pathway is technology. Today Grind has embraced RFID in a number of ways to remove friction. As new technology develops—near field communication, for instance—Grind must constantly be looking for ways to use that technology to remove friction. The last but most important pathway is community. The larger the community, the more useful it becomes to be a member. A large part of the Grind innovation map is to find ways to create more value for community members. That's what the Agora is all about. And there will be more in the future, I'm quite sure.

In terms of hard results to date, the first Grind location—called Grind 1—launched on September 6, 2011. After a year of planning and late nights and sawdust and headaches and debates and break-throughs, it was absolutely terrifying for the team to see if anyone would actually sign up. It turns out that they needn't have worried. Grind 1 was half full within two weeks. By the official launch party a month later, Grind 1 had over 130 paying members. By January 15, 2012, Grind 1 had over 400 members and had received requests from people to consider opening locations in Berlin, Amsterdam, London, São Paulo, Mumbai, Boston, Los Angeles, Seattle, Portland, Oregon, and Chicago. Grind has gotten coverage in *Fast Company, The Next Web, NY Convergence, Adweek, Architizer, Laughing Squid, Adafruit, PSFK, Co-Working It!, Workspace Design Magazine,* and *Inc.com.* It has been featured in a *Harvard Business Review* article about co-working, as well as the lead piece featured in a five-minute segment on CNBC. As of this writing, Grind 1 is full, with a lengthy waiting list for new members. Grind 2 and Grind 3 were under construction in Manhattan and Chicago, respectively, and the team is actively negotiating leases on additional locations.

Five Things You Need to Do to Synthesize *Your* Metastory and Create *Your* Action Map

Since every company's situation is different and every story is unique, it is a good bet that the situation you find yourself in is quite different than the situation Grind faced. Hopefully, the Grind case contains at least a few elements you can draw from personally, but there are also some general principles for developing an action map that should apply to any business and help you as you begin to translate your story into action.

1. Know your four truths and your metastory, and have your metastory understood by your senior managers. The importance of spending time on this step can't be overemphasized. Old habits die hard, and it is very easy to fall back into behaviors ingrained in the storytelling era—behaviors like moving directly to trying to communicate your story externally, rather than doing the work of translating your story into tangible actions. That work begins internally, and it takes time—it is very important to workshop the story throughout your organization, at least with leadership in key areas. This was done at Grind in a limited way with the founders, but it's a lot easier in a start-up. In a larger organization it may take multiple half-day and full-day workshops with different departments for folks to really understand what the metastory is for and how to use it. Remember, you're way ahead now, having read this book and gone through the process of arriving at your four truths and your metastory. It will take others in your organization a bit of time to catch up.

2 Plan to gather key managers from internal divisions and hold a series of at least half-day workshops where you take your metastory out for a test drive. You want to spend an hour or two engaging them in the process you have been through to arrive at your four truths and your metastory. You will also want to show them the action quad and get them familiar with each of the four areas. In advance, think through who is responsible for which quadrant. So, for instance, if you are meeting with the HR team, you will be concentrating on the *culture* quadrant of the action quad. Spend the last half of the session in a structured brainstorm, asking the attendees to imagine ways that the metastory might change the way they recruit employees or the way that employees are compensated and incentivized. The purpose of these sessions is to brainstorm new products, new services, and new behaviors that will help make the metastory real to internal as well as external participants. You are looking for new thinking and new ideas driven by the metastory, so make sure to capture the thinking in these sessions. But the more important goal in the early going is to get people used to the idea of thinking in this new way. If you are the CEO, great. If not, it helps to have folks present their findings from these sessions to the CEO. It's a real incentive to take the exercise seriously. And it's great for the CEO to see her people working with the metastory.

3 Once you have a healthy set of potential actions, explore changes that would need to be made to your internal processes and team structures to make these ideas happen. It's also good to give them a hard kicking from an economic standpoint. Financial analysis is a vital step for any major new product or business initiatives. It is best if these discussions are held with the company's top managers present, including your head of corporate strategy, CFO, and CEO, if possible. The discussions will reveal where the areas of real opportunity lie, and where the cost/benefit equation is going to be most favorable.

4. As in the Grind example, use the process to develop ongoing action principles. These are the rules of the road for each individual group or division to work against, moving forward. Though everyone will be working from the same metastory, each department should have its own specific set of goals and benchmarks. For example, HR should have its own distinct action plan for taking actions in their area that align with the metastory. Those actions will be different from those contained in the plan for R&D, but both sets of actions will align back to the metastory of the company.

5. Implement, learn, refine, and repeat. Some of your ideas will be easy to implement quickly. Others will take time. Start both, and work toward making them real. Storydoing is an ongoing process of discovery and refinement, not a "set and forget" kind of thing. Governance is key here. Define an internal cross-functional team that is tasked with ongoing support and monitoring of these initiatives and making sure that communication about successes, challenges, and learning is happening in both directions.

Conclusion

For a business to be competitive in the years ahead, it is important for an understanding of the metastory to exist at the highest levels inside that company. Embraced at these levels, the metastory can become the organizing principle for all business activity both inside and outside—pricing, product design, customer service, overall corporate quest, labor and hiring practices, and recruitment and retention policies. This means that the person most responsible for knowing the metastory and directing the coherent actions that tell the story is the CEO.

The Metastory as CEO

Venture capitalist Ben Horowitz recently declared, "A company without a story is a company without a strategy." His firm, Andreessen Horowitz, believes this is so fundamental to the success of the companies in which it invests that it has begun evaluating CEOs for their ability to articulate and guide the story of their companies. That is a game-changing approach and one that bodes well for the future of those start-ups.

But most of us don't work in start-ups. Most of us work in companies that were founded many years ago, in most cases by people who are present only as portraits on a wall somewhere, people we will never know. Often these people are spoken of in hushed tones, and terms like *visionary* are used to describe them. Respect and reverence for the past is good, but it won't help you run a company today or tomorrow. When some companies lose a founder, as we saw in the case of Shaklee, they seem to lose their way, as if the founder had been the keeper of a secret flame. Some companies, though, seem to make this leap and go on to thrive. Nike has had to go through this transition, and so far things look pretty good. JetBlue's founder has moved on, and the company seems to have retained an understanding of its metastory. When you encounter a business that really has a clear, institutional understanding of its metastory and is using it to drive all of its behavior, there is something palpably different about it. Companies like this stand out. When you think of it this way, it's not so much losing a visionary founder that's dangerous; the real danger is losing the understanding of the metastory that these leaders often carry inside them.

Some of the largest, oldest, and most successful companies in the world today got that way because they began with a clear and compelling metastory, one that became a tool of self-expression for millions of customers. I thought it might be useful to close the book with an example of a company that was actually created before the invention of television, grew to massive global success, went through the experience of losing the focus on its deeper metastory, and now seems to be on the verge of finding it again.

Kellogg's

Even if the only Kellogg's products you buy are Apple Jacks, Froot Loops, or Corn Pops, you're still likely to associate the company with one thought: better health through fiber. That thought is actually a vestige of the true metastory of the company, one that began over a hundred years ago, not with an ad campaign or with a cereal product, but with an innovative action. Two brothers, Dr. John Harvey Kellogg and Will Keith Kellogg, founded a spa devoted to health and wellness called the Battle Creek Sanitarium, in Battle Creek, Michigan. One of the important aspects of the sanitarium is that the Kellogg brothers were both local leaders in the Seventh-Day Adventist Church, and the sanitarium was originally funded by the church as a public service. So from the beginning, the Battle Creek Sanitarium had a powerful altruistic quest. It wasn't about making money; it was about pioneering the very latest techniques in physical fitness and holistic wellness and sharing the discoveries with others. John Harvey Kellogg was a respected medical doctor, and many of the original employees included some of the finest doctors, nurses, trainers, and fitness experts of the day. Many of them found the sanitarium quest so inspiring that they worked for little or no pay.

This cutting-edge health retreat advocated a vegetarian diet heavy in whole grains as well as exercise and fresh air. There were more exotic treatments like yogurt enemas, daily dips in electrified pools, and nights spent sleeping outdoors even in the Michigan winter. Canyon Ranch it wasn't. But many of the health ideas promoted by the spa were way ahead of their time and remain relevant and vital to this day.

The sanitarium's story spread, and it quickly became *the* place to go for the wealthy and the famous of the day, who flocked to Battle Creek to regain or improve their health. The Kellogg brothers hosted President Taft, Henry Ford, Mary Todd Lincoln, Roald Amundsen, Thomas Edison, George Bernard Shaw, Johnny Weissmuller, and Amelia Earhart, to name but a few.

To feed the throngs of visitors a healthy, fiber-rich diet, the brothers began producing their own foods, among them a variety of whole-grain cereals. One day, through a happy accident, the cereal team at the sanitarium discovered something new: cereal flakes. This novel breakfast experience quickly became one of the most popular items on the menu.

The brothers realized that, owing to the fame of the sanitarium, this innovation had a potentially massive audience as well as high commercial value. They decided to form a side venture to offer packaged, ready-to-eat "corn flakes" to people all across America. Eventually, their cereal would revolutionize the way people all over the world ate breakfast. But in the beginning, the cereal meant much more to people than a healthy breakfast. It was a way for people who couldn't afford the time or expense of a trip to the famed sanitarium to participate in the aspirational Kellogg metastory of modern holistic health and well-being. Eating Kellogg's cereal (and displaying Kellogg's cereal on your breakfast table) became a way of signaling your connection to the Kellogg's philosophy about living a modern healthy life. It also signaled a connection to the celebrities of the day—it connected folks to Kellogg's story and made them a member of this very exclusive tribe. Because of this, whole generations of Americans grew up with Kellogg's cereal in their lives.

In time, the cereal business grew to dwarf the sanitarium, which was hit hard by the stock market crash of 1929 and, like many of its well-to-do patrons, went bankrupt. What had begun as one small ingredient of a holistic, healthy lifestyle (cereal flakes) had blossomed in to a global, packaged-food company. Over time, the founding metastory of the business—Kellogg's as the pioneer of cutting-edge fitness and health practices—went into hibernation. Many of the people who bought Kellogg's cereals were not even aware that Kellogg's cereal had been invented at a sanitarium.

At this stage of development, a successful company often passes to a group of managers who focus on profitability, particularly if the company is publicly traded. People may take over who have less appreciation for the strategic imperative to maintain the original metastory. Some companies struggle at this point. This tension crept into the Kellogg's business pretty quickly in the 1950s and '60s when, as a result of the desire to grow still further, extremely sugary cereals were introduced into the product line. Cocoa Krispies, Apple Jacks, and Froot Loops were products with no apparent health benefits beyond that of the average pile of Halloween candy. They were clearly not part of the original Kellogg's metastory of health and wellness, yet they rapidly became huge businesses.

Off-story products, however profitable, can have a corrosive effect on a business, and Kellogg's is no exception. In addition to being almost antithetical to the founding metastory of the company, these sugary products had a second unintended effect: with their "candy" taste and cartoonish packaging clearly targeting kids, they began to create a wider social perception that cereal was for children. They introduced a *new* story about cereal that had nothing to do with health, and as a result many adults stopped eating cereal. The entire category suffered. Kellogg's US market share hit a low 36.7 percent in 1983. A prominent analyst called it "a fine company that's past its prime," and the cereal market was being regarded as "mature."[1] These comments convinced Kellogg's chairman at the time, William E. LaMothe, to take action. He reoriented the company back to adults, the 80 million baby boomers then in their thirties and early forties. Kellogg's introduced healthy new products, including Crispix, Raisin Squares, and Nutri-Grain Biscuits. In emphasizing cereal's nutritional value, Kellogg helped persuade US consumers aged twenty-five to forty-nine to eat 26 percent more cereal than people that age ate five years before. A return to the founding narrative restored Kellogg's to the path of growth and prosperity, a powerful indication of how, unless you have a healthy corn flakes business, Froot Loops really aren't good for your longevity as a company. This is a compelling reminder for all CEOs today that your company's metastory is your secret weapon.

As you look at Kellogg's products today, you can still feel the founding metastory in there. Corn Flakes, All Bran, Raisin Bran, Cracklin' Oat Bran, Special K, Product 19—all of these products continue to support it. And actions like acquiring Kashi and Bear Naked continue to add to at least part of its original metastory in a modern way. Most of the recent actions the company has taken suggest that Kellogg's thinks of itself as being exclusively in the food business: all of its acquisitions are in food; all of its new products are food. But if we use the metastory of the company as a guide, Kellogg's is actually a holistic healthy-lifestyle company that happens to have an incredibly robust food business. Which begs a question: Could Kellogg's begin to apply some of the lessons of storydoing to its business? Could Kellogg's unearth and carefully define its *full* original metastory, the story of being a holistic, healthy-lifestyle company, and use it to create an action map that would create new revenue opportunities *outside* of the food business?

That would open up some very interesting areas for innovation for Kellogg's. Today, for instance, technology and the internet would allow the original sanitarium to leave Battle Creek and come to a participant. So some very interesting questions for Kellogg's would be: What is the modern, web-based version of the Battle Creek sanitarium? How might Kellogg's use software, apps, and web-based content to create an immersive health-and-wellness system and community around its food products? And what new products or services might result from a return to doing the original Kellogg's metastory?

We actually see the beginnings of this in the new website Kellogg's has created for Special K. SpecialK.com allows women to set a diet or a health goal and then use tools at the site to track their progress toward achieving that goal. Clearly, this isn't a food product; it is a product/system that allows women to engage with Kellogg's products and, crucially, with each other, in a new way. It also expresses the original Kellogg's metastory perfectly.

Where might this lead? Kellogg's exercise clothing and equipment designed by today's leading fitness experts? A chain of Kellogg's health clubs? Kellogg's-owned sports teams or athletic competitions? Red Bull has already shown that all of this and more is possible. It comes down to whether current leadership is willing to listen to the original metastory or not. Today, they might define their competitive set as other food manufacturers. But if they listened to it, Kellogg's metastory would tell them that they actually have permission to become an authentic and credible competitor to a company like Nike. Following the principles of storydoing, Red Bull is the model for the future of Kellogg's, not General Foods.

Storydoing and Leadership

A very important aspect of making the transition from being a storytelling company to being a storydoing company is education and training. It needs to happen at all levels of an organization. But it needs to be modeled and led from the top of the company. This means that one of the biggest challenges that we face in business today is training the next generation of leaders. Through no fault of their own, many CEOs today often feel unprepared to think in right-brain or story terms. It's hard to blame them, since most often, they have a financial background, not a storytelling background. Leaders who have an appreciation for both right-brain and left-brain thinking are still quite rare at the highest levels in business. An appreciation for the power of story in business—an appreciation for the power of story to create shareholder value—is an attribute that *can* be taught, however.

We are beginning to see this happen at places like the Institute of Design at Stanford (the d.school), which has begun to embrace and train design principles as part of the business curriculum. This is a great start, but more must be done by business schools to foster and mentor a new generation of business leaders who can run the multidisciplinary teams necessary to create the story-led businesses of tomorrow. Jim Stengel calls these leaders *business artists*—people who combine the analytical and strategic skills of the traditional businessperson with the empathetic understanding and intuition of an artist or creative person.[2] I think that is a great term and something to which all of us should aspire. Whatever we call them, these new leaders will transform business over the next several decades. The era of decision making by dry, financial spreadsheet and management by PowerPoint alone is drawing to a close. To be great in business tomorrow, to create the great businesses *of* tomorrow, we must tap into something higher, something universally human and creative.

You probably don't have the luxury of time to wait for a new generation of leaders to emerge from business schools, however, and you shouldn't wait. You have a business to run right now. The truth is, you have the power to become an agent of change in your own organization today. You just have to roll up your sleeves and get to work.

If you are leading a company and are interested in pursuing the application of story-led action in your business, I hope some of the stories shared in this book have been helpful. One of the hardest things as a leader is to decide how much change your organization can withstand and to find allies and drivers within your organization to begin to implement that change. To test the waters, you might consider sharing some of the stories in this book with your top management team and get their points of view. Listen closely to the responses. They will tell you a lot about your team's ability to embrace change. Don't be disheartened if there are skeptics. That's a perfectly normal reaction to any discussion about change. But you may also discover some people who are excited by the prospect of transformation. Those people can become key evangelists in your culture, and you may want to consider giving them day-to-day oversight of an exploration of what that transformation could mean.

If you are not yet the leader, but an agent of change trying to figure out how to engage with the leadership of your company on this topic, you might also consider creating a presentation that shares some concrete examples of storydoing companies and the results they are achieving today. So long as this is presented as "provocative discussion fodder" and not "I have come to show you the future," you should be fine. Listen closely to the responses. They will tell you a lot about the kind of company you work in and how open to change the management truly is. Being an agent of change in a company where leadership isn't open to it is a recipe for frustration. Being an agent of change in a company where the leadership is open and supportive of new ideas can be one of the most satisfying experiences of your career.

One of the additional benefits of getting leadership as well as people from across your organization involved in a project like this is that the process itself creates collaborative habits within the company that will continue to bear fruit over time. Particularly in large businesses, this process will bring people together who may not have actually met each other or worked together before. The interaction can feel awkward at first, but it almost always results in new relationships and alliances that continue long after the project has been completed. The more collaborative and connected your company is, the better off it will be in the future and the better integrated your metastory will be in every action you make. One of the most compelling conclusions drawn from the 2012 IBM CEO survey, which surveys seventeen hundred of the top CEOs around the globe, is that companies with more collaborative cultures actually innovate faster and more effectively than those with more rigid and hierarchical cultures.[3] So for your company, this process can be like playing a sport you really love—it's fun, and can actually make you healthier at the same time.

Applying the Lessons to *Your* Business

We all live and work in a time when change in business is not something that is optional. And change in organizations does not come easily or without risk. Most people, given their preference, will stick with what they know. The same is true of organizations. I have spent nearly twenty-five years in the advertising and marketing industry, agitating for the new, the innovative, the next. So I naturally resonate with people who are dissatisfied with the status quo, people who are pushing or pulling their organizations toward the future. But it must also be acknowledged that it is still sweaty, uncertain work. One of the goals of this book is to remove some of the uncertainty inherent in change by laying out a practical process and tools that any businessperson can use.

It is fitting, then, to close with a few lessons learned along the way that apply to the implementation of the process covered in this book. Many companies hire outside consultants to help them with work like this, but there is no reason you can't do much of it yourself. What follows is not a formula. It is really a set of principles gleaned from experience. The process of getting at your own metastory and then creating your own action map does not involve retreating alone to a black box somewhere and then a triumphant return hours later to your boardroom with the answer. It's an organic process by necessity because, fundamentally, it is about discovery. Every company culture is different, so there is no one-size-fits-all approach. But there are a few specific things that you should definitely do (a few things you should definitely not do, too).

1. It's not a science—don't try to make it one. Anybody who tells you it's a science is lying to you. In the age of television,

for instance, research "science" told us that the only way to make an effective commercial was to say the name of the product in the first five seconds and repeat it as many times as possible before the end. Now ask yourself, what are some of your favorite commercials? Do they work that way? Now ask yourself what some of your favorite companies and brands are. Do their commercials work that way? My guess is none of your favorites work the way that research scientists said they should. Any good process is part art and part science. It should rely both on raw data and numbers as well as nuanced interpretation of those numbers. Humanity and gut feel matter.

2 Remember—storydoing is a team sport. You cannot do this alone. You need to build a cross-disciplinary team to accomplish this. You'll want to build a team that includes sales, IT or technology, R&D, finance, and whoever the key stakeholders are at the long-term strategy table for your company. Cross-disciplinary understanding and buy-in is critical to creating (and funding) real innovative action in any company. If you're not the CEO, then you need to make the CEO aware that storydoing is taking place and get him or her bought in to sponsoring this process, even as an experiment, in advance. If you're doing this right, you may ruffle a feather or two in your organization, so air cover is important.

3 Be honest. This sounds easy but turns out to be really hard when you discover something that is going to be unpopular or hard to fix. But approaching this process with a real sense of honesty and openness to both positive and negative discovery is crucial. If the product is lame, you need to be able to say it. If the Cleveland office is in the way, you need to be able to say it. If your own department is the one holding things back, you need to be able to say it. Dig hard for the truth and then stick to it. There is a lot of pressure inside organizations to get along and go along. But going along in the wrong direction isn't helpful to anyone. This does not mean you have to be difficult or rude. But at the end of the day, giving people what they are asking for doesn't help, unless it also happens to be what they *need*. You want to help, not please. If you don't have the air cover to be a truth teller in the organization, you won't make a lot of progress. It might be easier to look for a job in a company or a situation where that support does exist. They are out there.

④ Be generous. Getting to the core of the four truths is a collaborative process. The essence of collaboration is generosity. The best collaborators are confident enough in themselves and their talents not to need to have their opinion win the day, and especially not to get credit for having the opinion that won the day. Be generous with credit, praise, and communication—especially communication. People don't like change and can grow paranoid when the rumor mill starts to churn. When a stranger arrives to interview them about what they are doing and how they are doing it—with no communication in advance—they will make up all kinds of crazy stories about what is happening and why. A simple note from the sponsor to all interviewees in advance works wonders.

⑤ Know when to go outside for help. There is a reason that consultants exist. Sometimes it's just not possible for an insider to take the heat for delivering unpopular or jarring news. If it looks like it might get ugly, hiring an outsider who, if necessary, can take the bullet may be the best money you ever spent.

The five principles above will serve you well on your own quest of discovery and change. I will leave you with one final piece of advice: *remember to follow your heart.* Data is useful and important. But data will only get you so far. Stories live in the hearts of human beings. A lot of decision making based on gut feeling has been eliminated from big businesses today, to their detriment. The reason so many businesses feel so cold and aloof, so "corporate," is because people sense that the decisions being made are based on spreadsheets and not on advancing a coherent story.

There is a better way, a way that leads to greater sales and profits. That better way is empathy and a passion for helping people and improving their lives. Businesses that are passionate about making great experiences for people will win over time. Today the really monster successes are growing not from the question "How do we make as much money as possible?" but rather from the question "How do we make this a richer, more satisfying, more meaningful experience for people?"

That's my story and I'm sticking to it.

NOTES

Introduction

1. Teressa Iezzi, "Red Bull CEO Dietrich Mateschitz on Brand as Media Company," *Fast Company Co.Create*, February 17, 2012, www.fastcocreate .com/1679907/red-bull-ceo-dietrich-mateschitz-on-brand-as-media -company.

2. Ibid.

3. David Neeleman, JetBlue's internal mission statement, www.jetblue .com/flying-on-jetblue/customer-protection/.

4. US Census Bureau, WIPO, US Trademark Office, www.wipo.int/ ipstats/en/statistics/patents/.

5. "100 Leading National Advertisers Index," *Advertising Agency & Marketing Industry News*, http://adage.com/article/datacenter-advertising -spending/100-leading-national-advertisers-index/106348/.

6. John Gerzeman and Ed Lebar, *The Brand Bubble: The Looming Crisis in Brand Value and How to Avoid It* (San Francisco: Jossey-Bass, 2008).

7. James Allen, "Living Differentiation," HBR Blog Network, March 21, 2012, http://blogs.hbr.org/cs/2012/03/living_differentiation.html.

Chapter 1

1. Dee-Ann Durbin and Tom Krisher, "U.S. Auto Sales Up in September on Buys of SUVs and Pickups," *MassLive*, October 3, 2011, www.masslive.com/ business-news/index.ssf/2011/10/us_auto_sales_up_in_september_on_buys _of.html.

2. Mark Shaffer and Barak Goodman, "Rollover: The Hidden History of the SUV," *Frontline*, PBS, February 21, 2002.

3. There have been many interesting books, blogs, and papers written on this topic, but a particularly useful one, with a wealth of great source material in the bibliography, is a paper by Richard Elliot and Kritsadarat Wattanasuwan of Oxford University, "Brands as Symbolic Resources for the Construction of Reality," *International Journal of Advertising* 17, no. 2 (1998): 131–144.

4. *An Inconvenient Truth.* Directed by Davis Guggenheim. Produced by Laurie David, Lawrence Bender, and Scott Z. Burns. United States: Paramount Pictures Corp., 2006.

Chapter 2

1. comScore, "Next-Generation Strategies for Advertising to Millennials," www.comscore.com/Insights/Presentations_and_Whitepapers/2012/Next_Generation_Strategies_for_Advertising_to_Millennials, 2011.

2. "100 Leading National Advertisers Index," *Advertising Agency & Marketing Industry News*, June 2011, http://adage.com/article/datacenter-advertising-spending/100-leading-national-advertisers-index/106348/.

3. A. M. Bogusky and John Winsor, *Baked-in: Creating Products and Businesses That Market Themselves* (Chicago: Agate, 2009).

4. Carolyn Everson, "Social by Design" address to the Digital Marketing Exposition and Conference, Cologne, Germany, September 2011, http://vimeo.com/29398862.

5. Jessica Shambora, "How TOMS Shoes Founder Blake Mycoskie Got Started," *CNNMoney*, March 16, 2010, http://money.cnn.com/2010/03/16/smallbusiness/toms_shoes_blake_mycoskie.fortune/index.htm.

Chapter 4

1. All quotations for the Amplify case are from interviews by the author, September 6–November 15, 2011.

2. These included STAR (School Technology Action Report), Emerging Trends 2011, Xplana, Education and Technology Trends 2011, and the ASCD Top 5 Education Trends report.

3. There were numerous articles in the *New York Times* and the *Atlantic Monthly*. The team also consulted the *Wall Street Journal, Annals of Higher Education, Huffington Post* Education, *Chicago Sun-Times, America's Teachers on America's Schools* (published by Scholastic Inc.), and many other editorial sources.

4. Steven Brill, *Class Warfare: Inside the Fight to Fix America's Schools* (New York: Simon & Schuster, 2011).

5. *Condition of Education 2011* (Washington, DC: National Center for Education Statistics, 2011).

6. "Diplomas Count 2007: Ready for What? Preparing Students for College, Careers, and Life after High School," *Education Week*, June 12, 2007.

7. Education Week and the Editorial Projects in Education (EPE) Research Center, "Progress on Graduation Rate Stalls; 1.3 Million Students Fail to Earn Diplomas," Washington, DC, 2010.

8. *The Condition of College & Career Readiness 2010*, ACT, 2010, www.act .org/research/policymakers/cccr10/

9. *Education at a Glance 2011: OECD Indicators*, OECD, 69, http://dx.doi .org/10.1787/eag-2011-en.

10. Bureau of Labor Statistics, Department of Labor, "College Enrollment and Work Activity of 2010 High School Graduates" and "Employment and Unemployment Among Youth—Summer 2010," August 27, 2010, www.bls.gov/ news.release/archives/youth_08272010.pdf.

11. C. Rouse, *The Labor Market Consequences of an Inadequate Education* (Princeton, NJ: Princeton University and NBER); prepared for the Equity Symposium on "The Social Costs of Inadequate Education" at Teachers' College, Columbia University, September 2005.

12. Sandy Baum and Kathleen Payea, *Education Pays 2004: The Benefits of Higher Education for Individuals and Society* (New York: The College Board, Trends in Higher Education Series, 2004).

13. NCES Digest of Education Statistics, 2010 (NCES 2011–015), Table 188 and Chapter 2; NEA (Rankings of the States 2010 and Estimates of School Statistics 2011), www.nea.org/assets/docs/HE/NEA_Rankings_and_Estimates 010711.pdf

14. "eTForecasts (Computers-In-Use Forecast by Country)," US Census Bureau, www.etforecasts.com/products/ES_cinusev2.htm, and Institute for Education Statistics, *Teachers' Use of Educational Technology in U.S. Public Schools: 2009* (Washington, DC: National Center for Education Statistics, 2010), http://nces.ed.gov/pubs2010/2010040.pdf.

15. "eTForecasts (Computers-In-Use Forecast by Country)," US Census Bureau, www.etforecasts.com/products/ES_cinusev2.htm; and Harold Wenglinsky, *Using Technology Wisely: The Keys to Success in Schools*, 1st ed. (New York: Teachers College Press, 2005).

16. Project RED (Revolutionizing Education) is a research tool copyrighted in 2012 by The Greaves Group, The Hayes Connection, and the One-to-One Institute.

17. NCLB, Partnership for 21st Century Skills, 2005, www.p21.org/storage/documents/21st_century_skills_education_and_competitiveness_guide .pdf.

18. Cathy N. Davidson, *Now You See It: How the Brain Science of Attention Will Transform the Way We Live, Work, and Learn* (New York: Viking, 2011).

Chapter 5

1. Catherine Rampell, "As Layoffs Surge, Women May Pass Men in Job Force," *New York Times*, February 5, 2009, www.nytimes.com/2009/02/06/business/06women.html.

2. US Census Bureau, "More Working Women Than Men Have College Degrees, Census Bureau Reports," news release, April 26, 2011, www.census.gov/newsroom/releases/archives/education/cb11-72.html.

3. Michael Lewis, *Home Game: An Accidental Guide to Fatherhood* (New York: W.W. Norton, 2009).

4. Thomas Beller, *How to Be a Man: Scenes from a Protracted Boyhood* (New York: W.W. Norton, 2005).

5. Michael Chabon, *Manhood for Amateurs: The Pleasures and Regrets of a Husband, Father, and Son* (New York: Harper, 2009).

6. Matthew B. Crawford, *Shop Class as Soulcraft: An Inquiry into the Value of Work* (New York: Penguin Press, 2009).

7. Melanie Shreffler, *101 Charts about Men* (New York: EPM Communications, 2008).

8. *American Men: Who They Are & How They Live* (Ithaca, NY: New Strategist Publications, 2002).

9. Susan Mitchell, *Generation X: Americans Born 1965 to 1976*, 6th ed. (Ithaca, NY: New Strategist Publications, 2004).

10. *The Millennials: Americans Born 1977 to 1994*, 4th ed. (Ithaca, NY: New Strategist Publications, 2004).

11. Berkeley General Social Survey, http://sda.berkeley.edu/archive.htm.

12. Carmen DeNavas-Walt, Bernadette D. Proctor, and Jessica C. Smith, "United States Census Bureau: Income, Poverty, and Health Insurance Coverage in the United States 2010," September 2011, www.census.gov/prod/2011pubs/p60-239.pdf.

13. Fact Finder Survey for U.S. Labor Force, http://factfinder2.census.gov/faces/nav/jsf/pages/searchresults.xhtml?refresh=t.

14. Associated Press, "Domestic Violence on the Rise as Economy Sinks," April 10, 2009, www.msnbc.msn.com/id/30156918/ns/health-health_care/t/domestic-abuse-rise-economy-sinks/#.TzlxLZhuH18.

15. Amanda Lenhart, Kristen Purcell, Aaron Smith, and Kathryn Zickuhr, "Social Media and Young Adults, Part 2: Gadget Ownership and Wireless Connectivity," *Pew Internet*, February 2, 2010, http://pewinternet.org/Reports/2010/Social-Media-and-Young-Adults/Part-2/4-Gaming-devices.aspx.

16. *State of the Media: U.S. Digital Consumer Report, Q3–Q4 2011*, Nielsen, 2012, www.nielsen.com/us/en/insights/reports-downloads/2012/us-digital-consumer-report.html?status=success.

17. Kathleen Moore, "71% of Online Adults Now Use Video-sharing Sites," *Pew Internet,* July 26, 2011, www.pewinternet.org/Reports/2011/Video -sharing-sites/Report.aspx.

18. www.youtube.com/t/press_statistics.

Chapter 6

1. Jim Stengel, *Grow: How Ideals Power Growth and Profit at the World's Greatest Companies* (New York: Crown Business, 2011).

2. Shaklee Corporation, *Shaklee: What We're About* (Pleasanton, CA: Shaklee Corporation, 2011), http://images.shaklee.com/library/mission_ brochure_eng.pdf.

3. Basic H is a registered trademark of the Shaklee Corporation.

4. www.youtube.com/watch?v=j7OHG7tHrNM.

5. Jay P. Pederson, "Shaklee Corporation," in *International Directory of Company Histories,* vol. 39 (Detroit, MI: St. James Press, 2001).

6. Bureau of Labor Statistics, Department of Labor, "Employment and Unemployment Among Youth—Summer 2010," August 27, 2010, www.bls.gov/ news.release/archives/youth_08272010.pdf.

7. "Market of Ideas: Capitalism's Waning Popularity," *The Economist,* April 9, 2011.

8. "Let's Just Fix It. Forget Washington. Move Over, Mr. President. Every-day Americans Can Turn This Country Around," *Newsweek,* September 19, 2011.

9. "The BabyCenter 2010 Mom Social Influencer Report," June 14, 2010, www.babycenter.com/100_-the-babycenter-174-2010-mom-social-influencer-report-reveal_10332899.bc.

10. Elisa Camahort Page, "The BlogHer–IVillage 2010 Social Media Matters Study, co-sponsored by Ketchum and the Nielsen Company," July 2010, www.blogher.com/files/Social_Media_Matters_2010.pdf.

11. Aileen Lee, "Why Women Rule the Internet," *TechCrunch,* March 20, 2011, http://techcrunch.com/2011/03/20/why-women-rule-the-internet/.

12. BabyCenter's "21st Century Mom Report," June 29, 2009, http:// www.threedeepmarketing.com/wp-content/uploads/2010/02/BabyCenter _21stCenturyMom.pdf.

13. Ibid.

14. Ibid.

15. Robert L. Shook, *The Shaklee Story* (New York: Harper & Row, 1982).

16. Interview with the author, March 3, 2011.

17. Joan C. Williams, "The Three Faces of Work-Family Conflict: The Poor, the Professionals, and the Missing Middle," January 25, 2010, www.american progress.org/issues/2010/01/three_faces_report.html.

18. Scott Mayerowitz, "Americans Afraid to Take Full Vacations," *ABC News*, August 10, 2010, http://abcnews.go.com/Travel/americans-refuse -vacation-days-lag-rest-world/story?id=11361600.

Chapter 7

1. www.sustainablebusiness.com/index.cfm/go/news.display/id/18578.
2. www.sustainablebusiness.com/index.cfm/go/news.display/id/24279.
3. Co:collective analysis based on US Bureau of Labor Statistics, IDC, GAO (www.gao.gov/), and Richard L. Florida, *Cities and the Creative Class* (New York: Routledge, 2005). The analysis assumes 1.5x higher incidence of creative class among freelance and mobile workers than in the population as a whole.
4. Richard L. Florida, *The Rise of the Creative Class: And How It's Transforming Work, Leisure, Community and Everyday Life* (New York: Basic Books, 2002).
5. Carsten Foertsch, "Coworking in Manhattan, NYC," *Deskmag*, April 4, 2011, www.deskmag.com/en/coworking-spaces-in-manhattan-new-york-196.
6. Rachel Botsman and Roo Rogers, *What's Mine Is Yours: The Rise of Collaborative Consumption* (New York: Harper Business, 2010).

Conclusion

1. Patricia Sellers, "How King Kellogg Beat the Blahs: The Cereal Champ Lost Its Edge, Then Came Roaring Back. Now It Has Creamed Its Competitors and Brought New Life to a Business Everyone Said Was Mature," *CNN-Money*, August 29, 1988, http://money.cnn.com/magazines/fortune/fortune_ archive/1988/08/29/70950/index.htm.
2. Jim Stengel, *Grow: How Ideals Power Growth and Profit at the World's 50 Greatest Companies* (London: Virgin, 2012).
3. "IBM 2012 Global CEO Study," IBM Institute for Business Value, www .ibm.com/services/us/en/c-suite/ceostudy2012/.

INDEX

Index

Index

ACKNOWLEDGMENTS

I have always believed in the power of collaboration, but as a first-time author, the degree to which it takes a village to produce a book was a genuine revelation to me. Some heartfelt thanks are definitely in order.

First I have to acknowledge the help and inspiration of the clients whom we collaborated with on the projects contained in the book: Joel Klein, Kristen Kane, Diana Rhoten, and the whole team at Amplify; Niels Schuurmans, Todd Ames, and the whole team at Spike TV; Roger Barnett, Victor Barnett, and Brad Harrington at Shaklee Corporation; and Benjamin Dyett, Stuart and Karina Warshaw, and the extended community at Grind. Storydoers, all.

I'd also like to acknowledge the co:conspirators who worked with co: on several of the projects in the book: Scott Belsky and the team at Behance; Josh Rubin, Jose Mejia, and the whole team at Cool Hunting and Largetail; Andrew Zolty, Mike Lipton, and Mattias Gunneras at Breakfast; Josh Campbell at Magic+Might; Steve Farrell and the whole team at Smith; the incomparable Brian Clark and the whole team at GMD Studios; Doug Jaeger and Kristin Sloan at JaegerSloan; Felix Sockwell at Felix Sockwell Design; Graham Clifford at Graham Clifford Design; the tireless and inspiring Ernie

Schenck; Jeremy Sadler and the whole team at JDK design; Justin Luke at Audio Visual Arts; and Michael Ferdman and the incredible team at Firstborn.

I also have to give a shout-out to the whole team at co:collective, both those who kept other plates spinning while I worked on this project and those who contributed to it directly by driving the projects in the book forward. A few went above and beyond the call, including Jonny Chia and, in particular, Allie Dietzek. Go Honeybadgers!

I would be remiss if I failed to acknowledge three people who provided invaluable wisdom and guidance on the project: John Winsor, author and CEO of Victors & Spoils, and Brian Perkins, former CMO of Johnson & Johnson, who both contributed much-needed criticism and guidance on early drafts of the book; and journalist and author Stephen Williams, who did all the interviewing for the case histories and was an invaluable sounding board and coach throughout the project.

In the spirit of standing on the shoulders of giants, I'd also like to acknowledge some people whose work has provided inspiration and intellectual foundation for some of the ideas contained in this book: Peter Guber for his expertise in the craft of storytelling in general and specifically his HBR article on the four truths of the storyteller; and the team at Wolff Olins for laying the intellectual foundations for what we now refer to as the *action quad* in the book.

Finally, I have to thank my agent Jim Levine and the team at Harvard Business Review Press, including Ania Wieckowski, for believing in the idea for this book before we knew exactly what the idea was. And last but certainly not least, I owe a huge debt of gratitude to my brilliant and tireless editor Courtney Cashman for her counsel and collaboration.

ABOUT THE AUTHOR

TY MONTAGUE is a marketing innovator and agent of change who spent a twenty-plus-year career in advertising, first as a copywriter and then as a creative director at agencies including Chiat/Day, Bartle Bogle Hegarty, Wieden + Kennedy, and J. Walter Thompson. As Co-president and Chief Creative Officer of JWT North America, Montague and Co-president Rosemarie Ryan helped lead a five-year transformation of that agency that culminated with JWT being named Adweek's 2009 Global Agency of the Year.

In September 2010, Montague left the advertising business to launch a new company called co:collective with partners Rosemarie Ryan, Neil Parker, and Richard Schatzberger. Co:collective is a storydoing collective that specializes in inventing and reinventing businesses, brands, and products. Co: has been engaged by Google, MTV Networks, Microsoft, and News Corporation, among others.

Montague's advertising work has been recognized in every major creative competition in the advertising industry, including the International ANDY Awards, *The One Show*, Cannes, *Communication Arts*, D&AD, Clio, and the Effies. His work is also part of the permanent collection of the Museum of Modern Art.

Montague is a frequent speaker on the topics of creativity, story-telling, and innovation. He has been a guest lecturer at the Wharton School of Business, Columbia Business School, and the NYU Stern School of Business. *Creativity* magazine has named him one of the fifty most influential creatives of the past twenty years, and in 2010 honored him as one of the "Creativity 50"—celebrating "the most influential and inspiring creative personalities in the past year." In addition, *Fast Company* has included him as one of the Top Ten Creative Minds in business and featured him in a cover story as a business turnaround artist, and *Advertising Age* named him one of the Top 10 Creative Directors in America.

Montague grew up in Albuquerque, New Mexico, and today lives in Westport, Connecticut, with his wife, Dany, his son, Mack, and their beagle, Jerry.